The Natural History of

BUTTERFLIES

The Natural History of

BUTTERFLIES

JOHN FELTWELL

CROOM HELM
London

© 1986 John Feltwell
Croom Helm Ltd, Provident House, Burrell Row,
Beckenham, Kent BR3 1AT

British Library Cataloguing in Publication Data

Feltwell, John
  The natural history of butterflies.
  1. Butterflies
  I. Title
  595.78′9   QL542

  ISBN 0–7099–1059–2
  ISBN 0–7099–4905–7 Pbk

Phototypeset by Oxford Publishing Services
Printed and bound in Great Britain by Mackays of Chatham Ltd

Contents

Colour plates

1. A male silver-spotted skipper (*Hesperia comma*; Hesperidae) standing-
   by to fly off on a reconnaissance flight to intercept other patrolling
   insects. The skippers are unique in resting like this, with wings drawn
   back. They must have fairly universal wing joints which allows them
   so much manoeuvrability. When not waiting on standby like this, they
   raise their fore wings and bask in the sun. Strongly territorial they
   like a good 'dog-fight' (photographed at St Martial, Gard, France)

   (Please note that colour plate caption should read *Hesperia comma* and not *Ochlodes venata*)

2. The plain tiger (*Danaus chrysippus*) or African monarch has been
   increasing its range in southern Europe, from the Canary Islands and
   the Azores in the Atlantic to Spain and south-west France to southern
   Italy, Greece, and Corsica. Caterpillars store the poisonous
   cardenolides from the leaves of its milkweed (*Asclepias* spp.) food plant
   which provides protection for the chrysalis and adult. The bright
   colours of the butterflies are warning colours and are used as a model
   by several mimics (photographed in a butterfly house)

3. The apollo (*Parnassius apollo* : Papilionidae) is a beautiful butterfly
   from the mountains of Europe. It has black markings to help it absorb
   sunlight energy and its body has glycerides as an anti-freeze
   component. Sometimes its body feels 'greasy'. It can 'wink' at
   predators to scare them away by repeatedly moving the fore wings
   forward thus exposing and covering the false eyes. The apollo, and
   certain of its subspecies, is now protected in much of Europe. Many
   populations are threatened by human activities, such as forestry and
   tourism (skiing) (photograhed on Mt Lozère, Lozère, France)

4 The southern festoon (*Zerynthia polyxena* : Papilionidae) could be
   confused with its relative the Spanish festoon (*Z. rumina*) from Spain
   and Portugal, but not with the eastern festoon (*Z. cerisyi*) from eastern
   Europe including Greece and Crete. All three species use birthworts
   (*Aristolochia* spp.) as caterpillar food plants and their populations may
   be surprisingly large in the small habitats that they frequent
   (photographed at St Martial, Gard, France)

5. The Moroccan orange tip (*Anthocharis belia* : Pieridae) is a real teaser to photograph. Like the wood white and the Queen of Spain fritillary it is frequently so active that it never really settles down to a good drink of nectar for more than two or three seconds. It is drawn to the yellow flowers of buckler mustard (*Biscutella laevigata*) and *B. lyrata* from which it imbibes nectar and on which it lays its eggs. The colouring of the underside of the hind wings gives it excellent camouflage when at rest on these flower heads (photographed at St Guilhelm-le-Desert, Herault, France)

6. The wood white (*Leptidea sinapis*) patrols hedgerows, woodland margins and clearings where it will sometimes spend hours seeking out the right caterpillar food plants for egg-laying. A very dainty butterfly it is a feeble flier and may even be blown backwards if the wind is too strong. There are two other wood white species in Europe; the eastern wood white (*L. duponcheli*) and Fenton's wood white (*L. morsei*) (photographed in the Burren, western Ireland)

7. Black-veined whites (*Aporia crataegi* : Pieridae) can be exceedingly abundant and may reach pest proportions. They died out in Britain in 1925 and were successfully re-introduced for a few seasons by Winston Churchill. Butterflies become transparent due to increased sexual activity; females mate several times and each time the male holds onto her wings and rubs them. These two are fighting over the spoils of the scabious (*Scabiosa* spp.) flower in a meadow full of thousands of the butterflies (photographed on Causse de Blandas, Gard, France)

8. The brimstone (*Gonepteryx rhamni* : Pieridae) is well known amongst lepidopterists and laymen alike. It is often the first and last to be seen each year. It may have given rise to the name of 'butterfly' since it is butter-coloured and common throughout its range. In southern Europe it overlaps, and is eventually replaced by, the magnificent cleopatra (*Gonepteryx cleopatra*). The brimstone hibernates as a butterfly and has an excellent leaf-like outline ideal for winter refuge in a bank of ivy-leaves. This one was photographed in October having spent the night, somewhat unwisely, on a thistle head. This, the north side of the butterfly, was covered in dew drops, the south side was clear of dew-drops and was warming up nicely. The photograph was taken by flash, thus the black background. The next night it probably went into hibernation (photographed at Friston Forest, east Sussex, England)

9. The 'not-tonight-dear' response exhibited by the female of the small white (*Pieris rapae* : Pieridae). This is a behaviour characteristic seen in several butterfly species which indicates to prospective male suitors that the female does not want any sex. Although some butterflies mate several times, the raised abdomen indicates that the female does not wish to mate at this moment. It is sometimes confused for a 'yes, I am willing' attitude (photographed at St Martial, Gard, France)

10. An expert at audio-visual defence, the peacock (*Inachis io* : Nymphalidae) has very large vertebrate-like false eyes and makes a rustling sound with its wings. The undersides of the peacock are dark

for camouflage, but when disturbed it opens its wings and reveals these bright colours. The effect is to startle predators. Repeated opening and closing emphasises the pretence. The peacock is a common butterfly in gardens where its caterpillars feed on nettles (*Urtica* spp.) (photographed at Henley Down, east Sussex, England)

11. The painted lady (*Cynthia cardui* : Nymphalidae) is a powerful migrant which regularly moves throughout north-west Europe from centres of overpopulation in North Africa. It has several caterpillar food plants but thrives well on thistles (*Cirsium* spp.). A fresh female like this with swollen abdomen full of eggs may have just arrived from the Continent without too much damage to its wings (photographed at Henley Down, east Sussex, England)

12. The southern white admiral (*Ladoga reducta* : Nymphalidae) is fairly similar to the more northerly-living white admiral (*L. camilla*) in pattern but the upper surfaces of its wings are covered with a delicate purple sheen. The underside is distinctive with more white at the base of the hind wing. The white admiral is a July flier in England (it is the logo of the Sussex Trust for Nature Conservation), but the southern white admiral flies from May to September. Both species lay eggs on honeysuckle and are found in oak woods, or in open scrubby areas with oak (photographed at St Martial, Gard, France)

13. The silver-washed fritillary (*Argynnis paphia* : Nymphalidae) is a magnificent woodland butterfly. Like so many of the fritillaries the caterpillars are dependent upon woodland and wayside violets. Unlike the other fritillaries the female of this species lays her eggs on the bark of tree trunks close to violet clumps. The butterflies rely on clearings, glades and forest edges for day to day survival since they gather to feed on a large variety of flowering plants. Their orange colours are very distinctive in the sunshine. The butterflies have an elaborate courtship ritual which still needs to be investigated further (photographed at Col de L'Homme Mort, Gard, France)

14. Now a protected species in Britain, the heath fritillary (*Mellicta athalia* : Nymphalidae), is a threatened butterfly with only a few localities left. On the Continent it is widely distributed and sometimes common. The butterflies live in woodland glades and scrubby areas where its food plants cow wheat (*Melampyrum* spp.) and plantain (*Plantago* spp.) occur. It has been re-introduced several times in England with some limited success. The word 'fritillary', like the name of the plant refers to its spotted nature (photographed at St Martial, Gard, France)

15. The male common blue (*Polyommatus icarus* : Lycaenidae) is both very common and very blue on the upper surface of its wings. The underside reveals a complex pattern of variable spots and colours which has been the subject of several investigations. Males of several species of blues gather at drinking spots, such as damp sand enriched with animal urine or on animal dung to top up with minerals needed in manufacturing their complex insect hormones. Males may settle on

your skin to imbibe sweaty salts (photographed at St Martial, Gard,
France)

16. The long-tailed blue (*Lampides boeticus* : Lycaenidae) is one of those
    few animals which almost has a worldwide distribution. Typical of
    many of the blues it rests for the night with its head down on
    vegetation. It is a strongly migratory butterfly, quite common in
    southern Europe, and is very occasionally found in southern England.
    Like the scarce swallowtail, it has evolved a back-to-front mimicry
    with its false eye spots and long 'tails' to deceive predators. The
    caterpillars often feed on leguminous plants in the garden (photo-
    graphed in Bogor, Java, Indonesia)

17. The black satyr (*Satyrus actaea* : Satyridae) is almost black on its
    upper surface, except for a single white eye spot on the fore wing. It
    can be exceedingly abundant in flowery meadows above 1,000 m and
    its dark colours serve it well for absorbing the sunlight energy
    (photographed on Mt Aigoual, Gard, France)

18. One of the many mountain ringlets, this is the Arran brown (*Erebia
    ligea* : Satyridae). All the erebias have the same sort of pattern of
    brown wings with reddish bars containing variable numbers of spots.
    They are a favourite group of mountain butterflies to study and can be
    very elusive flying with ease across scree, rock walls and around
    mountain tops. Their dark colours help them to absorb the sun's
    energy. The caterpillars feed on several species of grass and, in several
    species, go through two winters before they are fully grown. One of the
    risks of feeding from flowers is the danger from predatory spiders, as
    in this butterfly (photographed on Mt Aigoual, Gard, France)

19. The scarce copper (*Heodes virgaureae* : Lycaenidae) is not particularly
    'scarce' in southern Europe; in fact it can be very common along
    waysides. The bright colours of the male glinting in the sun are easily
    seen whilst motoring. Note how the speckled female has completely
    different colours; a good example of sexual dimorphism. Like the small
    copper (*Lycaena phlaeas*) the caterpillars feed on docks (*Rumex* spp.)
    (photographed on Mt Lozère, Lozère, France)

20. The green hairstreak (*Callophrys rubi* : Lycaenidae) is a pugnacious
    little butterfly which gathers in groups in suitable warm spots.
    Several may patrol a small corner, moving between perch points, and
    chasing any other insect which enters its air space. It flies in the
    spring and the green camouflage colours of the undersides serve it well
    for life amongst fresh green spring leaves. The uppersides are dull
    brown. Note how the butterfly has positioned itself side on to the
    sunlight. It does this specifically to absorb more sunlight energy
    (photographed at St Martial, Gard, France).

Figures

Tables

Acknowledgements

Many thanks are due to Michael Tweedie, Geoffrey Burton and George Else who have been exceedingly helpful in reading the text and making useful comments. My good friends in France, Jacques and Denise Lhonoré, Yves Maccagno and Patrick Ducros have sympathised with my entomological interests over the last eighteen years and have accompanied me to some very interesting butterfly habitats. Miriam Rothschild has always been ready to listen to my ideas and has encouraged me with comments and suggestions.

I am grateful to the Royal Entomological Society of London for permission to reproduce Table 8.1 from *The Biology of Butterflies*, Miss Pamela Gilbert of the British Museum (Natural History), Mrs B.G. Leonard of the Royal Entomological Society for helping me with my research, Helen Senior and Valerie Baines for their excellent artwork. All the colour photographs were taken by the author, much of it on Fujichrome film, for which the author is very grateful to Hanimex (UK) Limited.

Preface

This book is about the natural history of butterflies in Europe and North Africa. It presents a collection of essays on those interesting aspects of butterflies' lives; how they live, how and why they have marvellous colours, how they court, interact with wild plants and the sunshine, migrate, choose habitats, defend territories and build up populations. It is also about the ecology of butterflies and their conservation. This is the first time that some subjects like habitats have been looked at in such depth. The book does not give details of the distribution of all butterflies or delve deeply into butterfly genetics since these two important topics have been dealt with admirably by others. Instead it acts as a companion to those two great works: Higgins and Riley's *Butterflies of Britain and Europe* and Ford's *Butterflies*. Over 200,000 copies of Higgins and Riley's book and the recent companion pocket book are now in circulation in the nine countries in which it has been translated. Ford's book is a classic; a third of it is devoted to butterfly genetics and evolution.

I have tried to present the book in a popular manner to reach the growing number of people who study butterflies as a hobby. The common names of butterflies and plants are followed by their Latin names where they are mentioned for the first time in each chapter. A bibliography has been included for those who want further information. Although several people have commented on the draft manuscripts, I take full responsibility for the contents and ideas. This is simply a personal look at butterfly natural history; there is no doubt that we are only just beginning to understand the ecology of butterflies.

John Feltwell

To my parents for the French connection and Cumnor House School for encouraging my early natural history interests on Ashdown Forest

1 Historical

Oh! pleasant, pleasant were the days,
The time when, in our childish plays,
My sister Emmeline and I
Together chased the butterfly!
A very good hunter did I rush
Upon the prey: with leaps and springs
I followed on from brake to bush;
But she, God lovlier! feared to brush
The dust from off its wings

Charles Waterton (1871) *Essays of a Naturalist*

FOSSIL BUTTERFLIES

Butterflies probably came into existence about 150 million years ago at about the same time as flowering plants. It is likely that there has been a constant co-evolution between wild plants and butterflies since they have been found fossilised together in the same deposits in the early Cretaceous (Table 1.1). It is thought that caddis flies (Order Trichoptera) and butterflies and moths (Order Lepidoptera) evolved from a common ancestor since present-day examples share similarities. There is a family of small moths called the Micropterygidae which have biting mouthparts like the aquatic larvae of the caddis flies. These provide the evidence which suggests there is a link. It is now clear that butterflies evolved from moths. The primitive moth feature of hooking the wings together is retained in at least one species of butterfly, and then only in the male, of the Australian skipper (*Euschemon rafflesia*).

Very few butterfly fossils exist in the world; in fact only 41 had even been recorded by 1976. This is because their delicate wings and soft bodies are not as hard as the tough wing cases, or elytra of beetles or the harder wings of dragonflies of which we know a little more. At least 80 insect species have been recovered from coal measures of the late Carboniferous period. The oldest fossil insects were like present-day cockroaches recorded from the Upper Devonian deposits west of the Urals (USSR). They had wingspans of about 40 cm. The big fossilised dragonflies from Europe and America were late Carboniferous (about 300 million years ago) and the

1

Table 1.1 Geological time scale

Million years ago	Name	Era
0	Present	
2	Pleistocene	
7	Pliocene	
26	Miocene	Tertiary or Cenozoic
38	Oligocene	
54	Eocene	
64	Palaeocene	
136	Cretaceous	
193	Jurassic	Mesozoic
225	Triassic	
280	Permian	
345	Carboniferous	Palaeozoic
395	Devonian	

earliest Lepidoptera early Cretaceous (about 120 million years ago), so the dragonflies pre-date the butterflies by about 180 million years. By the lower Oligocene (35 million years ago) many of the different families of butterflies had evolved. The fossils appear to be like present-day members of the skippers, browns, apollos, yellows and whites, snout butterflies, nymphalids and one is like a lycaenid.

Much of the original research on fossil butterflies was carried out by the American Samuel Scudder (1837–1911). In his words:

'The happy discovery in the Museum of Marseilles of a new fossil butterfly first drew my attention to this group of extinct insects . . . I was able to study not only all the originals of the Museums of Aix, Marseilles, Zurich, Paris, London, Cambridge and Warwick but several new types described here for the first time.'

Samuel Scudder clearly identified nine butterflies in Europe, all derived from Tertiary deposits no more than 65 million years old. The gypsum deposits of Aix-en-Provence proved to be the most productive, but fossils had also been found in Austria and Prussia (a former German kingdom).

Nymphalid-like butterfly fossils have subsequently been found in Europe. Just before Scudder's work, Butler at Oxford had described a fossil nymphalid from Stonesfield slate. Fossil nymphalids were then described in 1965 from rocks and sandy deposits of the north Caucasus. The only other butterfly fossils which have been found in Europe are a lycaenid and swallowtail species from the coastal limestone of Gabbro in Italy and a 'white' from south-west Germany.

Several of the fossil butterflies show a remarkable similarity to present-day butterflies. The Vienna Museum preserves *Papilio pluto*, perhaps the oldest forebear of the European swallowtail (*Papilio machaon*). There is no doubt that the basic food plants of many of the butterflies were around at this early period, such as members of the cabbage (Cruciferae), grass (Graminae) and pea family (Leguminosae).

Some butterflies have been found preserved in amber, the fossilised resin from trees. It is produced as an insect deterrent and somehow, probably by accident, the insects became stuck, enveloped and eventually fossilised in it. Baltic amber is a noted source and the 'blue-earth amber' from the Samland region of east Prussia is dated to the Oligocene period. John Evelyn, roving emissary of King James I and English diarist of the seventeenth century, described how, in Milan, he visited the private museum of Signor Septalla, a canon of St Ambrose and was shown 'much amber full of insects'.

One way or another two swallowtail-like butterflies and an unidentified lycaenid caterpillar ended up fossilised in Baltic amber dating from the Upper Eocene (about 50 million years ago) and the Lower Oligocene. These are among the earliest Lepidoptera known. Other butterflies belonging to the whites and nymphalids have also been found in Africa. More recently the scales of a micropterygid moth have been found in amber in the north-west of France. In Canada the head of a caterpillar found in amber is complete with most features, such as jaws and simple eyes. There is also the plant material present which indicates that the caterpillar lived in a leaf tunnel and may, therefore, have been a primitive moth. Nevertheless, it is the earliest known Lepidoptera from Cretaceous deposits — slightly earlier than the European amber insects — at 72 million years old.

BUTTERFLY HUNTERS IN EUROPE

Very little is known about butterfly collecting trips in Europe in the seventeenth century although there were some books published on insects generally. John Evelyn visited many museums, gardens and private collections when he was in France and Italy in the seventeenth century. An entry in his diary for 1644 recalls a visit he made to the garden and collections of a Monsieur Morine in Paris:

'His collections of all sorts of insects, especially of butterflies, is most curious: these he spreads and so medicates, that no corruption invading them, he keeps them in drawers, so placed as to represent a beautiful piece of tapestry . . . and one butterfly resembling a perfect bird.'

The eighteenth century was dominated by Carl Linnaeus's (1707–78) work in classifying animals. He devised the binominal system of nomenclature whereby all living creatures were given two Latin names, the first, or generic name, followed by the second or specific name. He placed all butterflies into the genus *Papilio* which is now divided into separate butterfly families on the basis of differences in genitalia and wing venation. Little did he realise that these names would change many times over with the continued scrutiny of naturalists' eyes or that national museums would be set up to deal with this diverse flora and fauna. His own collection is now housed in the special environment of the strongroom of the Linnaean Society in Piccadilly, London where his 200-year-old specimens still look remarkably fresh. What Linnaeus left every naturalist worldwide is a sensible way of talking about species using just one language; understood by all nations. His works were so well approved by the Swedish royal family that he was honoured by them; in fact Queen Lorisa Ulrika became a close friend and she too collected butterflies.

Unfortunately we do not learn much about butterflies from the famous naturalist Gilbert White (1720–93) of Selborne at the end of the eighteenth century. This is disappointing since there must have been plenty of woodland butterflies in the forest of the Weald that he would have seen in his travels in the south of England, but he was more an ornithologist than an entomologist. Surprisingly, fritillaries, white admirals (*Ladoga camilla*) and purple emperors (*Apatura iris*) are not mentioned. White casually noted that butterflies were good food for wheatears and he passed some other comments on aphids, flies, dragonflies, mayflies, beetles and bumble bees.

Jean-Henri Fabre's name is synonymous with insects. Born in 1823 he was a contemporary of Charles Darwin and the two corresponded. He must have been familiar with the butterflies of the south of France, particularly of the Nîmes garrigue, the Cévennes mountains to the west and the Rhone valley where he eventually settled. He was professor of mathematics at the Imperial College of Ajaccio in Corsica for four years but he had a keen interest in all forms of nature and published 95 books; 30 of them when he lived near Orange in Provence. He died in 1915 aged 92. Fabre — the insect man — is perhaps more familiar for his writings on solitary bees, cicadas, beetles and moths than he is for butterflies. Today his carefully conserved private study is just like a Victorian naturalist's den; he collected everything. Charles Darwin was fourteen years Fabre's senior and died in 1882 aged 73. On butterflies, he discusses mimicry of tropical butterflies in his *Origin of Species* and mentions the work of one of his contemporaries, Mr Bates. Henry Bates gave his name to one form of mimicry called Batesian mimicry but this is not seen in any butterfly species in Europe; only in a pair of moths — the white and buff ermines (*Spilosoma lubricipeda, S. lutea*).

Another Frenchman, Louis Pasteur (1822–95) studied moths rather than butterflies. Towards the end of the nineteenth century he was called to the Cévennes by public subscription to deal with a disease of the silkworm (*Bombyx mori*) called the *pébrine*. As an expert on bacterial diseases he was able to give advice in selecting hardy stock and thus solving the problem.

The Englishwoman, Margaret Fountaine (1862–1940), travelled extensively in Europe. She visited France, Germany, Greece, Hungary, Italy, Syria and Turkey, though from her writings she seemed more preoccupied with amorous affairs than with butterflies. Some of her descriptions of habitats are interesting as they shed light on abundance of butterflies and on the Victorian mentality for collecting. For instance, in Turkey, in the Tschírtschir Valley, at the end of June 1903 'the road was a dream of *Lycaenas* . . . there was *L. hopferi* and *L. menalcas*, also *L. poseidon*, in such abundance that we would go back day after day with some fifty, sixty or even seventy specimens in my collecting box.' Or, in Hungary with members of the Budapest Entomological Society in 1898: '. . . after more than two hours of bumping and jolting along we arrived — an entomologist's dream realized, a forest abounding with butterflies, the *suvarovius* flying by hundreds, a white graceful creature; *M. aurelia, A. daphne, P. alciphron* (purple shot copper) and *C. morpheus* (large chequered skipper); butterflies rare in other localities were abundant here.'

In Sicily in 1896 she befriended at Palermo 'the well-known entomologist' Signor Emile Ragusa (1849–1924) who told her of the whereabouts of the Sicilian subspecies of the western marbled white (*Melanargia occitanica pherusa*). Today this is only known from Sicily where it is very local. The following year Miss Fountaine visited Vienna to see the entomologist Baron Adolf von Kalchberg (1841–99). He put her in pursuit of the lattis brown (*Kirinia roxelana*), a butterfly of the mountainous Balkans where today its food plant is still not known. On top of the mountains she also found the *P. clymene* . . . on the lower ground she was pleased to bag the common glider (*Neptis sappho*), an eastern European nymphalid.

Another intrepid lady lepidopterist was Mary De La Beche Nicholle (1839–1922) who did a lot of butterfly collecting throughout Europe between the 1880s and early 1900s. She made expeditions to the Balkans, Bulgaria, France, Spain, Italy, North Africa and Switzerland. She lived in Wales and kept diaries of her entomological observations and much of this is used as the basis of a book on her. One of her eccentric trade marks was that she used an ear trumpet!

Like many Victorians she collected lots of series of butterflies and was enthralled by trophies such as alexanor (*Papilio alexanor*) at Digne in the South of France, or the spring ringlet (*Erebia epistygne*) around Les Dourbes. On her travels she met many butterfly collectors, like Lord Walsingham, collectors for Otto Staudinger (1830–1900), Henry John Elwes (1846–1922), Josep Haberhauer an expert on Bulgarian butterflies, Professor Maximillian Korb (1851–1933) and, in 1902 in Algiers, Miss Margaret Fountaine.

Her exploits in Bulgaria make interesting reading. She went on a camping expedition and named the various camp sites after certain features; for instance, 'Cynthia' camp (probably after the abundant Cynthia's fritillary, *Hypodryas cynthia*), 'Erebia' camp after the mountain ringlets, 'bear' camp after a roaming bear and 'ghost' camp after the ghost swift moths which swirled around the camp light.

The Russian lepidopterist Vladimir Nabokov (1899–1977) wrote about the butterflies he loved; he collected in Russia and the Swiss alps and in the words of Miriam Rothschild:

'Nabokov's greatest gift was not the presentation of the Purple Emperor in our dream net, but the miraculous capture of that elusive period of childhood which imprints the countryside with its scents and sounds and sunlight and shadows in our bones rather than our minds.'

Nabokov spent most of his time working in the United States (where his novel *Lolita* made him famous) but he eventually named twelve new species and subspecies, including Nabokov's Pug. His poem *A discovery* eloquently describes the rewards of naming a species new to science.

Probably the greatest advancement in the study of European Lepidoptera, if not of the world, came through the energies of Walter Rothschild. During his 69 years from 1868 to 1937 he had 250 collectors working for him. In 1936 his collection of over 2,000,000 butterflies and moths, housed in the specially-built museum at Tring (Hertfordshire) was given to the Trustees of the British Museum. The collection contains thousands of original specimens of new species from which detailed descriptions were published. These are called 'type specimens' and are very important for research on insects. They now form the basis of the British Museum (Natural History) collection — now called the Rothschild-Cockayne-Kettlewell collection — and make it the foremost place in the world to study the classification of butterflies.

Between 1893 and 1908 Walter Rothschild had collectors working in Belgium, Corsica, the Caucasus mountains of south-west USSR, Cyprus, Finland, France, Holland, Ireland, Jordan, Norway, Poland, Spain,

Switzerland and Syria and Turkey; along the North African coast in Algeria, Morocco and Tunisia and on the Atlantic islands of the Azores, Canaries and Madeira. Unfortunately much of his correspondence has been burnt — a Rothschild custom — so that precious information on habitats, species and abundance has been lost. Many of these collectors were employed full-time by Walter Rothschild; for instance Victor Faroult collected and bred Lepidoptera for him in Algeria. Butterflies and moths were only a tiny part of what was collected for Walter's museum at Tring; beetles, mammals, birds and fish were also exceedingly well represented.

Walter himself departed on a long expedition in 1908 which took him through North Africa and into the Alps. He reported that: 'By the time we get back if all is well we shall have collected in 6 months over 15,000 Lepidoptera, about 4,000 other insects, 80–85 mammals, and 376 birds — an achievement that cannot easily be equalled in the Palaearctic region.'

In Switzerland he had managed to amass 5,191 Lepidoptera: 'I think a record anywhere as Wallace's collection during his Malay Archipelago trip of several years was not 6,000.' He was equally proficient at the moth light, collecting 1,167 moths of about 70 species in one night in mid-July 'a seething struggling mass of moths such as I suppose was never seen before in Europe'.

Walter's younger brother Charles also collected in Europe. His Hungarian collection was probably the largest Hungarian material ever collected in that country. Miriam Rothschild recounted the story of how he pulled the communication cord of the Dabes train as he wanted to chase a rare butterfly he had just seen from the carriage window. Charles is also credited with having promoted the establishment of the Puszta Nature Reserve where collecting is strictly controlled.

European countries were very thoroughly scoured by the intrepid butterfly-collector Baron Charles de Worms (1903–76). His unmistakable figure and his annual reports about his entomological journeys will always be remembered by lepidopterists. He was probably one of the first highly mobile lepidopterists who used the motor car for getting from one locality to the next. He visited the mountains of the Alps and Pyrénées, in Greece he was amongst the first to find two butterflies previously not recorded west of the USSR and Asiatic Turkey, the pontic blue (*Agrodiaetus coelestinus*) and the damon blue (*Agrodiaetus damon*). The Atlas mountains in Morocco — themselves a fairly unworked area in Europe — proved rewarding for the collector Colin Wyatt in 1974. Here is one of the most restricted butterflies in the world, Vogel's blue (*Plebejus vogelii*) only found in Morocco at one pass in the Middle Atlas.

Dr Lionel Higgins (1891–1985) made a lot of collecting trips in Europe and North Africa. With his colleague, Norman Riley (1890–1979), he produced the most comprehensive and celebrated book on the identification and distribution of European butterflies, *Butterflies of Britain and Europe* (1970). Higgins was a family doctor, specialising in gynaecology and obstetrics, whilst Riley devoted about 60 years working at the British Museum (Natural History). It is said that entomologists live a long time; these two proved the point.

2 Structure and function

'Crawling at your feet,' said the Gnat (Alice drew her feet back in some alarm), 'you may observe a Bread-and-butterfly. Its wings are thin slices of bread-and-butter, its body is a crust, and its head is a lump of sugar.'

Lewis Carroll (1832–98) *Alice in Wonderland*

BUTTERFLIES AS INVERTEBRATES, ARTHROPODS AND INSECTS

Butterflies are invertebrates. They all lack a backbone and may be soft- or hard-bodied with signs of segmentation. Invertebrates outnumber vertebrates by 30 to 1. There are about 1,500,000 species of invertebrate already known on Earth, and it is estimated that an amazing total of between 2 million and 10 million wait to be discovered and described. Most of these will undoubtedly be insects.

Butterflies belong to the class Insecta which is a division of the phylum Arthropoda. So, by what features do we recognise an arthropod or an insect?

All arthropods have six things in common. They are enclosed in a tough exoskeleton made of chitin; they are segmented; they have legs or other appendages arising from separate segments; they have a body cavity called a haemocoele (the area between the exoskeleton and the internal organs); they have a dorsal contractile heart; and a ventral nervous system. There are of course exceptions to this general plan, such as a lack of legs or wings. All insects have five major external characteristics, but they are not all necessarily visible in the adult insect. Some of the characteristics are only seen in early stages. There is much modification of the basic insect plan and there are plenty of exceptions.

The body of an insect is divided into three parts: the head, thorax and abdomen; this is clearly seen in most butterflies and moths. There are usually two pairs of wings but there are plenty of parasitic or primitive insects which do not have or need any. There are usually three pairs of legs but in some butterflies there may be only two functional pairs. There is one pair of antennae. On the side of the body are tiny pores which are called spiracles through which the insect breathes.

7

The Order Lepidoptera

Butterflies belong to the order of insects called the Lepidoptera. This comes from the Greek meaning that the wings are covered in scales (*lepis*, a scale; *pteron*, a wing). Butterflies share this characteristic with moths. There is enormous variety in the shape of butterflies' scales and it is well worth the while looking at them under a microscope. Scent scales, or androconia are modified scales with long drawn out ends found on male butterflies. Every scale has many minute longitudinal corrugations rather like the shape of corrugated iron. The number is very variable per scale, but these ripples are very important in producing the metallic colours from sunlight as seen in the blues and copper butterflies.

The Order Lepidoptera is divided into the butterflies (sub-order Rhopalocera) and moths (sub-order Heterocera). This division of the Lepidoptera is based on one of the principal characteristics of butterflies, that they have clubbed or knobbed antennae. *Rhopa* is Greek for a club or horn. Similarly the word Heterocera comes from the Greek meaning 'with different antennae'.

The antennae are sometimes called feelers, but this indicates that they are involved with touch and feeling. Although they do have sensitive hair receptors their principal function is as a 'nose' with a powerful sense of smell. The grandness of the antennae is often a reflection of their great powers of smell — especially for detecting distant mates. Under the scanning electron microscope the surface of antennae is rather like a sponge with plenty of pores into which the volatile insect pheromones and the subtle odours of wild plants can fall and be detected.

Butterfly or Moth?

The question is always posed, what is the difference between a butterfly and a moth? There are some simple guidelines but be warned, there are plenty of exceptions which break these 'rules'.

However, for our purposes we can list six differences:

1. Butterflies have knobbed antennae, moths do not.
   Exceptions: look at the swollen antennae of the day-flying burnet moths (*Zygaena* spp.).
2. Butterflies fly during the day (diurnal), moths at night (nocturnal).
   Exceptions: there are numerous day-flying moths and some butterflies have been recorded at moth lights.
3. Butterflies have bright colours, moths have dull colours.
   Exceptions: many browns and skippers are dull (see dingy skipper, *Erynnis tages*); many day-flying moths have bright butterfly colours.
4. Butterflies rest with their wings vertically clapped above their bodies; moths rest with theirs horizontally on their bodies.
   Exceptions: many skippers rest with their wings at different angles, many geometrid moths rest with wings open or clapped together.
5. Butterflies do not have such hairy bodies as moths.
   Exceptions: butterflies are often as hairy as moths, especially those that live on the cold upper slopes of mountains, e.g. the apollo butterflies (*Parnassius* spp.).
6. Butterflies do not have tiny hooks or bristles which link fore wing to hind wing as in most moths.
   Exceptions: there are no European butterflies which have hooks on

Figure 2.1 Head of typical butterfly showing pair of knobbed antennae, compound eyes and curled proboscis

their wings. This is therefore a useful characteristic but the hooks are so small that you would have to have a hand lens to see them.

Butterfly Families

Butterflies in western Europe are divided into nine separate families according to their structure. Note that many of the butterfly families may be called by their anglicised Latin name, e.g. nymphalids, pierids, and so on. Snout butterflies should not be confused with snout moths belonging to the family Noctuidae. Two of these families only have one species represented in western Europe: the snouts and the metalmarks; the monarch family has two species in Europe. But what characteristics have we used to separate each family from another? The pattern of the wing veins is the most reliable method though the general structure or 'looks' of the butterfly are sometimes sufficient to an experienced eye.

Coloration is a useful guide too and is used to describe some of the families such as whites, browns and blues. But beware, in some species males are completely different in colour from females and a few were originally classified as separate species. Individual variation of spots, lines and patterns can cause identification problems too.

Skippers. Wings are about as long as their whole body length; broad head and thorax and widely separated antennae. This family is thought to be relatively primitive. There are about 40 species in Europe.

Swallowtails. Large wings with or without a 'tail', colours and patterns are usually bright and distinctive. The functional significance of the butterfly's 'tails' is dealt with in Chapter 5. There are about 11 species in Europe.

Figure 2.2 Large skipper in characteristic resting position

Whites and Yellows. Large white or yellow wings with black spots. Tips of legs end in four claws instead of two. There are 41 species in Europe.

Monarchs. Large orange-brown wings with white spots, caterpillars with two pairs of black horns at either end of body. Caterpillars and adults store poisons from the food plant. There are two species in Europe, the monarch (*Danaus plexippus*) and the plain tiger (*Danaus chrysippus*).

Snouts. Named after the long forward projection from the head which is most pronounced when seen from the side. There is only one species in western Europe, the nettle tree butterfly (*Libythea celtis*) which is a representative of many more in tropical Africa and Asia.

Brush-footed butterflies. Also called aristocrats after their rich aristocratic colours and aristocratic names. Called brush-footed butterflies since their first pair of vestigial legs are tucked up under their 'chins' and are covered in hair. Nearly all of the fritillaries are included in this family (except the Duke of Burgundy fritillary). The nymphalids share the feature of having only four functional legs with the browns and the male of the Duke of Burgundy.

Browns. Mostly brown butterflies (except the marbled whites, *Melanargia* spp.) which have swollen veins at the base of their fore wings. Their caterpillars are tapered at both ends and may have a divided 'tail'. Some caterpillars hibernate twice. There are 113 species in Europe.

Metalmarks. There is only one species in Europe, the Duke of Burgundy fritillary (*Hamearis lucina*). The sexes differ structurally; the female has six functional legs, the male only four.

Blues, coppers and hairstreaks. Many have flashy metallic colours, particularly in the male, the female being a dull brown colour. They have short wings and some have banded antennae and legs. Some may have very short 'tails'. There are many more blues than hairstreaks. Hairstreaks are so named because of the fine lines they have across the underside of the hind wings. There are about 100 species in Europe.

Table 2.1 Butterfly families

Common names	Latin families
Skippers	Hesperiidae
Swallowtails	Papilionidae
Whites and yellows	Pieridae
Monarchs	Danaidae
Snout butterflies	Libytheidae
Brush-footed butterflies	Nymphalidae
Browns	Satyridae
Metalmarks	Nemeobiidae
Blues, coppers, hairstreaks	Lycaenidae

Compound Eyes and Vision

Caterpillars and butterflies have completely different eyes; and both are based upon a completely different system from those of vertebrates. In the caterpillar there are batteries of tiny simple eyes or ocelli (sometimes called stemmata) at the side of the head.

Butterflies have a pair of compound eyes on either side of the head. They are made up of several thousand lensed-eyes called ommatidia. Unlike many other insects they do not have a triangle of ocelli on the top of the head. Their compound eyes help the insect generally to appreciate their immediate surroundings and to detect movement. They cannot see precise detail but are able to detect if a predator is too close. They would know something was near them, but could not tell detail, such as the difference between one type of insectivorous bird and another. Their sight is made up of a complex mosaic of pictures.

There are about 6,000 ommatidia in each compound eye of a butterfly. The more ommatidia in an eye the greater the power of detecting prey, so that aerial carnivores like dragonflies have about 30,000 in each compound eye.

Light passes down each ommatidium and between the pigmented sides down to the nerves at the base where an impulse is carried off to the brain. As in most insects the brain is 'programmed' to set off a flying/moving/crawling/jumping reaction when a certain number of ommatidia are stimulated during a fraction of a millisecond. So the insect responds as if it has programmed behaviour only if the threshold of stimuli per unit time has been exceeded.

Butterflies obviously see colour. That is why many of them are so brightly-coloured. Several species, like the orange tip (*Anthocharis cardamines*), common blue (*Polyommatus icarus*) or purple emperor (*Apatura iris*), are sexually dimorphic which means that the sexes have different colours. Generally males are flashier than females, but there are exceptions.

The colour spectrum that man can perceive goes from red to indigo. Insects can do much better. They can see further into the violet end of the spectrum, into an area which contains ultra-violet light. Ordinary daylight has plenty of ultra-violet light and plants have made good use of it through evolution. Since insects see ultra-violet as a colour (which is invisible to us) some flowers have evolved a pattern in terms of this 'colour'. That is to say some parts of the petals reflect ultra-violet, others absorb it. Usually the parts that absorb it form a pattern that guides the insect to the nectaries. These patterns are sometimes called 'honey-guides', though 'nectar-guides' is more correct.

Honey-bees (*Apis mellifera*) rely on nectar guides to direct them quickly to the source of sugary secretions. It is a symbiotic relationship between insect and plant where both parties derive benefit; the insect food, the plant pollination. Butterflies and moths have cashed in on the same reward system but their role in pollination is not regarded as being very great. Work in Germany has shown that, in the large white butterfly (*Pieris brassicae*), at least, the female changes her colour preference with age. When freshly emerged she prefers a variety of different coloured flowers, from red to blue for nectar sources, then when she is ready to lay eggs she selects yellow to blue plants (like those of cabbages).

Ultra-violet light is not only absorbed on petals. It is also differentially absorbed onto butterfly wings for a very important purpose; so that sexes can recognise each other. If a pair of white butterflies is photographed in the presence of ultra-violet light (such as that from one of the mercury vapour bulbs used for collecting moths) the pictures will show clear sexual differences. These surprising differences make it possible for butterflies to tell each other apart when, to the human eye, they look very similar.

In pierids orange and greenish areas on the wings and andronial patches on the male's fore wing reflect more of the ultra-violet light than elsewhere. In species like the brimstone (*Gonepteryx rhamni*) and green-veined white (*Pieris rapae*) it appears that sexual recognition is achieved primarily by this visual method. Gerard Chovet demonstrated this quite clearly with his experiments in Paris. He used model female brimstones rotated at ten revolutions per minute, simulating the wing beats, and males were attracted to them.

Legs for Movement and Finding Food Plants

Caterpillars have many more legs than the butterflies they will eventually become. In fact the first three pairs of legs behind the head are called the true legs since they are the precursors of the more complicated legs which will appear in the same place in the butterfly. In the middle of the body are four pairs of prolegs which are larger and modified for gripping onto leaves and twigs. At the rear of the caterpillar are a pair of claspers which can grip the surface so strongly that it is sometimes difficult to remove a caterpillar from its food plant. Both the prolegs and the claspers have series of tiny hooks around the extremities and they are used for keeping a good purchase on supports.

The three pairs of butterfly legs arise from each of the thorax segments. They are long and thin and made up of distinct parts. The base of the leg is the coxa, followed by the femur, tibia, tarsus, claws and pads. Each major part is articulated together since they are an extension of the outer hard skeleton and contain muscles. The restrictive exoskeleton can be regarded as a suit of armour. Movement is only accomplished with movement at the joints. At the tip of the legs are claws which help to hold on to plants or rocks on landing or walking.

The extremity of the leg is a very important area. It is here that a host of sensory receptors lay hidden in the tarsi of the foot. These are specialised cells which are able to take an instant reading of the chemistry of the substrate. This is very important for the egg-laying females since they have to locate their correct food plants quickly. The receptors act like a mobile chemistry laboratory analysing the chemical difference between, for instance, two related food plants. If you watch butterflies you will notice that they will fly in close to plants, momentarily touch them, and pass on if it is the wrong species. During this brief half-second encounter they have successfully analysed the make-up of the plant.

Wings for Flight, Ornament and 'Love-dust'

Attached to each of the two rear segments of the thorax are a pair of wings. During metamorphosis they appear as clearly delineated areas on the outer case of the chrysalis. While the chrysalis is maturing the wings become visible through the cuticle until the colour and pattern is quite obvious a few hours before hatching.

When a butterfly emerges from a chrysalis it has very small and soft wings which have to be pumped up to full size. This is done by flooding the wing veins with blood (haemolymph) and pumping in air. Sometimes the wing joints can be seen leaking small amounts of yellow blood where excess escapes from the system. When the wings are full size the cuticle dries hard making an effective wing membrane. If the butterfly is disturbed during this time by a predator the wings may become crippled. The tough veins spread over the wings as a framework on which the thin cuticle containing scales is borne.

The surface area of the butterfly wing varies greatly from tiny wings of skippers or the small blue (*Cupido minimus*) to large surface areas of the swallowtails. Flapping the wings provides lift upwards and thrust forward. During flight the forces of drag act behind and gravity pulls from below. Both these forces have to be overcome by lift and thrust.

The wings provide a surface area for coloration and a place to carry some of the encapsulated smells used in courtship behaviour. All the scales on the wings are arranged in neat overlapping rows, each has a special peg at its base which fits neatly into a socket in the wing framework. All butterflies and moths hatch out with a complete collection of scales — probably up to one and a half million in some species — but these start to fall off the wings from the moment it starts flying. The clap of each wing beat sends showers of scales into the air — this is clearly seen in high speed cine-photography of butterfly flight.

Some of the scales are highly modified as scent capsules, especially in males. On the fore wing of several species, are dark areas or bands, called sex brands where these androconia are present. These are particularly visible in species like the large skipper (*Ochlodes venata*), gatekeeper (*Pyronia tithonus*) and silver-washed fritillary (*Argynnis paphia*). During courtship the male tries to get these 'scent bombs' as close as possible to the female. They break at special weak points and release a shower of particles which are commonly called 'love-dust'. The pheromones released by the male at the female are thought to have an aphrodisiac action on her.

The Abdomen for Breathing and Reproduction

Butterfly abdomens are usually long and relatively thin. Along the sides of the thorax and abdomen are tiny pores which are present on most of the segments. These are the spiracles which allow air to pass into a system of reinforced tubes called the tracheoles. Oxygen from the air is exchanged for carbon dioxide, a product of respiration. There is no direct pumping system, rather a slight dilation of the spiracles as the insect moves, or as the caterpillar (which also has them) walks.

The blood system is an open system. This means that there is no closed pumping system and complete set of different diameter tubes for circulating the blood. The analogy to a radiator system and boiler does not exist in any insect. Instead they have a dorsal blood vessel (a long thin heart) which is open at both ends. This is clearly visible along the 'back' of some caterpillars with transparent cuticles and you can see the blood being pushed with dilations to the front. Blood flows out of small holes in the heart, called ostia, of which there is a pair in each segment. The blood which comes out at the front end of the body gradually makes its way to the rear again to complete the system. It allows all the body organs to be bathed in blood.

This open system is very efficient for small creatures like insects, but it is absolutely hopeless for larger creatures. They need a closed system of tubes and a large pump. For this reason it is impossible to evolve any enormous insects by natural selection, without changing to a closed system. Science fiction writers take note! The largest and longest insects in the world are atlas moths (*Attacus atlas*), which have 26 cm wingspans, and exceptionally long stick-insects. Nothing bigger can ever be evolved in an insect.

Unlike vertebrates, the nervous system of insects runs along the underside of the body, rather than along the top or 'back'. It sends nerves into each segment and is continuous with the brain. Insect brains are highly complex organs; those of honey-bees have been shown to be exceedingly complicated but little work has been done on butterfly brains. What we can gather from the behaviour of insects, however, is that much of what insects do is governed by previously programmed patterns of response built into the brain. Insects react to stimuli all the time. They do not think and are not intelligent, though they may appear to do intelligent things.

The abdomen contains the reproductive organs, testes in the male and ovaries in the female. These organs start to develop in the caterpillar but are impossible to see in most living specimens. Occasionally the testes can be seen as a pink shadow through the body wall on the underside of a fully grown caterpillar.

Some male butterflies extrude a collection of bristles from the abdomen. These are called hairpencils and are used to distribute volatile smells used in courtship. One butterfly which has been studied is the monarch or milkweed the large immigrant from North America. The bristles are quite large in proportion to the abdomen and are retracted when not in use. A butterfly can sometimes be encouraged to evert the hairpencils with a little gentle pressure on the abdomen. There are several moths of the family Noctuidae which also possess hairpencils and some grasshoppers extrude scent brushes from their legs. Further study on these structures should yield fascinating results regarding courtship and attraction in butterflies.

The chemical substances released from androconia or from hairpencils are highly volatile. Other sex scents released from females of the oak eggar (*Lasiocampa quercus*) can be detected by the male at distances of up to 1.7 km downwind. The power of detecting these pheromones or insect hormones is more highly developed in moths since, being nocturnal, they have to rely on their sense of smell. Even so, butterflies probably detect their mates and their food plants up to several hundred metres away downwind.

Pheromones play a vital role in courtship rituals of butterflies — in other words preparing them for mating. Pheromones are highly complex chemicals which have the effect of altering the behaviour of an insect. It may have a stimulating or a deterrent effect and they may be produced by either sex.

When a virgin female insect hatches out she produces a large amount of pheromone which attracts males downwind. Males get a fix on the direction of the female since their two antennae give a directional reading. It is quite likely that several males will arrive on the scene at the same time to contest possession of the female. In some species it has been shown

Figure 2.3   Hairpencils extruded from abdomen

that males then let off a pheromone aimed at competitors, which has the effect of deterring the ardour of these other contestants. The fittest male comes through this chemical haze of pheromones and then launches another pheromone attack on the female, this time with an aphrodisiac action. What precisely goes on in the immediate vicinity of the courting butterflies is always difficult to assess, since it is very difficult to grab small parcels of air and quantify the contents.

Smell is important for sexes to find each other and may be the first stimulus that a potential mate receives. When in sight of his quarry visual cues become important. Coloration is the subject of Chapter 5.

3 Life cycles

A caterpillar it had been,
Once clad in suit of nature's green;
But now how changed by nature's laws!
Where are the eyes, the legs, the jaws? . . .
Lo! the shrouded thing . . .
Unfolding rises from each side;
Its tapering form in beauty dressed,
Like gold dust o'er a yellow vest
Whilst hands unseen had giv'n the power
To gather sweets and suck the flower,
It is a butterfly, as bright
As ever sparkled in the light.

H.G. Adams (1881) *Beautiful Butterflies*

INTRODUCTION

This chapter is all about butterfly metamorphosis; how butterflies develop through a series of stages from the egg to the adult. Special emphasis is given to the ecological relations that each stage has with its environment and with other animals. Hibernation is dealt with in each stage and details of courtship in the butterfly are given. The terminology used here (and throughout this book) follows the popular terms for each stage — egg, caterpillar, chrysalis and adult or butterfly. A more scientific language favours ovum(a), larva(ae), pupa(ae) and imago(imagines), but frequently the two sets of terminology are interchanged.

EGGS

Butterfly eggs come in all shapes and sizes, are laid singly or in groups, overwinter or hatch within a few days and are packed with nutrients or laced with deterrent poisons. Butterflies are either born with their full complement of mature eggs or the eggs mature gradually inside them.

The shape of butterfly eggs is sometimes a useful identification key to the family, for instance eggs of the blues, coppers and hairstreaks are flattened and disc-shaped, whilst those of the whites are tall and thin.

Many butterfly eggs have a characteristic pattern of sculpturing on their shells. This is so unique as to be of some considerable use in identifying butterflies solely by looking at the eggs. But beware, other insects have similar sized and coloured eggs; for instance the eggs of the Colorado beetle (*Leptinotarsa decemlineata*) and the large white (*Pieris brassicae*) look very similar in size, colour and the way they are laid in groups.

Sculpturing may take the form of longitudinal keels (or ridges) and furrows radiating out from a central area, called the micropyle. This fine aperture is where respiration takes place for the developing egg. Other patterns take the form of a lattice.

Eggs risk being eaten by true bugs (Hemiptera) and beetle larvae (Coleoptera) and being parasitised by hymenopterous egg parasites. The strategy in most butterfly species is to produce eggs which are concealed from predators and parasites. Most butterfly eggs are fairly drab coloured. One exception to this is the eggs of the white butterflies, which tend to be yellowy-orange and showy. The pigments which make them yellow are carotenoids. These are derived from the caterpillar's food plant and passed to the butterfly via the chrysalis. This implies that carotenoids are passed via the ovaries into the eggs. Carotenoids are vital to most animals since they can be converted into vitamin A which aids in growth and vision. It is noticeable that in species like the large white the newly hatched caterpillar eats its egg case, thus gaining vital nutrients. If caterpillars like the speckled wood (*Pararge aegeria*) are denied eating their egg case they will die.

The colour of eggs sometimes changes with age. As the caterpillar develops inside, the light colour may change to a richer colour and eventually give way to a dark colour in which the minute caterpillar is just visible. The heavily toughened jaws of the caterpillar may appear a rich chestnut or black colour.

Butterflies exhibit minimal parental concern for their offspring. The best thing they do for their young is to place the eggs on the right food plant, or near to it. Some, like the marbled white (*Melanargia galathea*) and ringlet (*Aphantopus hyperantus*), do not bother to do this. They broadcast their eggs whilst flying. The philosophy here is surely that as grasses occur very widely the chances of the eggs coming to rest on them is pretty high. This is obviously a system which works well but appears to carry a high risk. In direct contrast, other members of the brown butterfly family lay their eggs singly on grasses and rushes. The silver-washed fritillary (*Argynnis paphia*) is unique amongst European butterflies in laying its eggs close to its violet food plants, in fact, on the bark of trees. The newly hatched caterpillars have then to locate and walk to their food plants before they have their first meal.

There is some evidence that in the large white butterfly females have a preference for laying eggs on food plants that they themselves grew up on when they were caterpillars — a sort of chemical imprinting. In the holly blue (*Celastrina argiolus*), at least, the idea that the female butterfly is guided by a 'memory' of what she fed on as a larva is disposed as the butterflies have two generations on two different food plants each year.

Locating the correct caterpillar food plant is a major preoccupation of most female butterflies. Eggs may be laid on either the upper or lower surface of the leaf. Below the leaf the eggs are less liable to be damaged by sunlight and are out of the gaze of predators. When females lay eggs they

Table 3.1 Some butterflies which overwinter as eggs

Essex skipper	(*Thymelicus lineola*)
Silver-spotted skipper	(*Hesperia comma*)
Apollo	(*Parnassius* spp.)
High brown fritillary	(*Argynnis adippe*)
Silver-studded blue	(*Plebejus argus*)
Silvery blue	(*Aricia nicias*)
Chalkhill blue	(*Lysandra coridon*)
Idas blue	(*Lycaeides idas*)
Brown hairstreak	(*Thecla betulae*)
Purple hairstreak	(*Quercusia quercus*)
White-letter hairstreak	(*Strymonidia w-album*)
Black hairstreak	(*Strymonidia pruni*)
Scarce copper	(*Heodes virgaureae*)

produce a material which glues each egg to the surface of the leaf. This hardens and secures the egg in place. The glue is absent in those species which lay their eggs in flight. It has been speculated that the female is able to impart a pheromone to the eggs which is released and acts as a deterrent substance to predators.

Butterflies like the cabbage white lay their eggs in batches. Careful inspection shows that they are precision laid in neat rows. This accuracy of laying while facing the other way must be accomplished by the use of sensory hairs on the tip of the abdomen of the female. The large white seems to lay her eggs equally on the upper and lower surfaces of leaves. The small tortoiseshell (*Aglais urticae*) does not bother with neat and tidy rows. She lays hers as a pile of several scores of eggs on stinging nettle (*Urtica* spp.) leaves. The map butterfly (*Araschnia levana*), which also lays her eggs on nettle, does so as strings which hang from the undersides of the leaves. Professor E.B. Ford drew attention to nine British species of butterfly which lay their eggs in groups of 100 or more and five species which lay theirs in batches of 5 to 15. Most with large egg groups belong to the nymphalids.

Eggs either remain dormant soon after they are laid and overwinter as 'diapausing' eggs or they hatch within a few days. There must be a mechanism for determining whether the egg continues development or suspends its development over winter. Both amount of light per day (photoperiod) and temperature almost certainly regulate development.

Whilst eggs are developing they may be parasitised by small parasitic wasps called *Trichogramma evanescens*, which lay several eggs inside each butterfly egg and the larvae develop within. In some parts of eastern Europe *Trichogramma* has been used as a method of biological control against plagues of cabbage whites; thousands have been reared and deliberately released.

With such a high mortality of eggs from parasites and predators butterflies have evolved a strategy of producing lots of eggs. Some are supposed to lay over 500 eggs but the average number is thought to be between 200 and 300. In captivity the silver-washed fritillary will lay up to 600 eggs, the clouded yellow (*Colias croceus*) 500 and the small tortoise-shell batches of 80 to 100 eggs.

CATERPILLARS

Caterpillars are the principal feeding stage in the life cycle of a butterfly and it is during the caterpillar stage that an insect does all its growing. Many are rather like non-stop eating machines with few breaks for resting. In order to get bigger the caterpillars have to shed their skins. This is done during a process called ecdysis.

Before ecdysis can start the caterpillar has to seek a suitable place away from danger. The old skin is peeled back from the top of the head where the split occurs. The caterpillar is vulnerable at this stage as the new skin is very soft and provides no support for movement. By swelling up from the inside the caterpillar is able to expand its new skin until it sets hard. There are usually four such ecdyses during the caterpillar stage. Each caterpillar stage is called an instar. The first instar caterpillar hatches out of the egg and then through a series of four ecdyses it eventually becomes a fully-grown fifth instar caterpillar.

Butterfly caterpillars are much easier to identify than those of moths since there are considerably fewer of them and they are fairly distinctive. Caterpillars either have background matching colours or bright warning colours (see Chapter 5). As they get older their colours and patterns can change dramatically making identification difficult.

Whilst feeding, caterpillars have to cope with attacks from predators and parasites. They have evolved an interesting variety of ways of deterring or avoiding predators. One method is to try and keep out of sight. This is done either by having background matching colour or living perpetually on the undersides of leaves. But the undersides of leaves are not always a safe place. Titmice (*Parus* spp.) are very good at checking-out all sorts of nooks and crannies. Many of the Lycaenid caterpillars are flattened from top to bottom and their slug-like forms look almost as though they are gliding over the surface of the leaves and buds which they resemble.

Another good avoidance strategy is to look like a bird dropping. This is a widespread practice in some swallowtails (*Papilio* spp.) of south-east Asia but is not found in many European butterflies. The comma (*Polygonia c-album*) is a good example. Its caterpillars have blotches of white on their spiny bodies and in the last instar the back end of the caterpillar is completely white. The small caterpillar of the poplar admiral (*Ladoga populi*) also looks like a bird dropping; the chrysalis of the black hairstreak (*Strymonidia pruni*) looks like one too. Despite this, researchers have shown that up to 90 per cent of them are still detected and eaten by birds in some species.

The use of defensive spines is seen in many butterfly caterpillars, especially the nymphalids. Spiny caterpillars may also live together for safety in numbers. If a bird alights on a leaf, the caterpillars all stop feeding and, if disturbed further, will throw up their heads violently. This may be accompanied, as in the caterpillars of the small tortoisehell and peacock (*Inachis io*), with regurgitation of a liquid from the mouth. This acts as a deterrent to drive the bird away.

Caterpillar spines also help to make it difficult for parasitic wasps to find a purchase for egg laying. Combined with violent body movements the parasite may be deterred. However, the highly successful ichneumon fly (*Apanteles glomeratus*), manages to attack first and second instar cater-

Figure 3.1   Caterpillar of purple emperor camouflaged on leaf

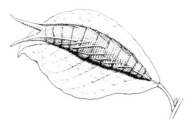

pillars, and can inflict very high mortalities on butterfly populations, especially those of the large white.

A gregarious way of life clearly has its advantages. But there are butterflies whose caterpillars are distinctly solitary. There are advantages in being single: more food and less chance that other members of the same family group will become parasitised or eaten at the same time. In the wild, caterpillars have the chance to space themselves out and there are fewer adverse interactions, but in captivity caterpillars of the orange tip (*Anthocharis cardamines*) become cannibalistic.

The European swallowtail (*Papilio machaon*) uses a unique method amongst butterflies to deter predators. When disturbed it everts a pair of orange 'horns' from its head; the more disturbed the further these bright osmateria are extruded and waggle around. They arise from the top of the head and the first few segments of the caterpillar become hunched up, drawing attention to these waggling 'horns'. The osmateria also produce a strong smell, which is possibly a deterrent to parasites.

Some caterpillars defend themselves in or on silk. Those of the red admiral (*Vanessa atalanta*) and painted lady (*Cynthia cardui*) live a solitary existence inside a leaf which they draw together with silk. Others, like the small tortoiseshell and marsh fritillary (*Euphydryas aurinia*) and the Granville fritillary (*Melitaea cinxia*), spin silk over their food plant and live in a communal web. The Assmann's fritillary (*Mellicta britomartis*) in Sweden hibernates in its specially thickened communal web as do those of the marsh fritillary. They all derive some safety in numbers. The caterpillars of the black-veined white (*Aporia crataegi*) are well equipped to ward off predators, since they live communally, have poisonous hairs and give off a deterrent odour.

Some of the skipper caterpillars live safely inside the long leaves of

Figure 3.2   Fully-grown caterpillar of the swallowtail with its osmateria everted

grasses which are drawn together by silk. These species include the Lulworth skipper (*Thymelicus acteon*), large skipper (*Ochlodes venata*), small skipper (*Thymelicus sylvestris*) and chequered skipper (*Carterocephalus palaemon*). Feeding at night and resting during the day avoids any contact with birds. This is done in the meadow brown (*Maniola jurtina*), ringlet and wall (*Lasiommata megera*). During the day the caterpillars hide in the confined space at the bottom of grass clumps.

When caterpillars become fully grown they finish feeding and become restless. Their general colour becomes a little faded and they set off for a period of 'wandering'. Their dulled colours afford them some protection from predators. It seems that it is a physiological requirement of many caterpillars to go through this stage of wandering in preparation for pupation. If they are being kept in a shoe-box they will walk round repeatedly before settling down to pupate. In the wild, caterpillars will wander up to 100 m from their food plants and will cross fields and roads. It is during the wandering stage that many caterpillars are first discovered — crossing the road or garden path — well exposed to the elements and predators. There is even a case of a plague of large white caterpillars in Russia leaving a cabbage field and crossing a railway line — they were crushed and brought trains to a halt!

Caterpillars of many members of the blues, coppers and hairstreaks family (Lycaenidae) have associations with ants. This a common phenomenom of the Lycaenidae family worldwide. The story of the large blue (*Maculinea arion*) caterpillar's association with ants is not unique; but the demise of the large blue in England in 1979 focused national attention on the curious way of life that these caterpillars have evolved.

The association of a butterfly and ant is a reciprocal relationship where both parties derive some benefit. It is called symbiosis. The caterpillar gets complimentary board and lodgings safe from predators, and the ants get a hand-out of a tasty secretion each time they stimulate the caterpillar. Ants 'milk' aphids and practice aphid farming too; looking after them in winter in their galleries and putting them on suitable juicy stems in the spring.

Through evolution the large blue has associated itself with one genus of plant and one species of ant. Its caterpillar food plant is thyme (*Thymus* spp.) and its particular ant species is *Myrmica sabuleti*. Other species of ant live in butterfly habitats but only this species prefers the short turf. Whilst the young caterpillar is feeding on the thyme, it is apprehended by a roving *sabuleti* ant which stimulates it to produce a 'milk' from the honey-gland on the seventh abdominal segment. On sating its appetite the ant takes the caterpillar off to the safety of its ant colony, where the caterpillar feeds on ant grubs (expendable in quantity) and the ants receive in return, 'milk' on demand. The caterpillar hibernates in the galleries, resumes feeding in the spring, pupates in a gallery and crawls to the surface immediately on hatching. It has a delayed wing-expansion programme to allow it to find its way out of the maze of galleries and on to a secure twig above ground, without becoming crippled.

The large blue apparently became extinct in England in 1979 due to an upset in the ecological balance of its West Country habitat. I use the word 'apparently' since there are those people who believe that the species still survives in a secret locality. An upset in the state of the rabbit was a major influencing factor in the extinction of the large blue. With rabbits dying off due to myxomatosis, the grass grew long and eliminated the short grassland turf much liked by the *sabuleti* ant, which supported the caterpillars. The long grass also obscured the thyme plants on which the females lay their eggs. This was despite the fact that thyme often grows on the top of ant hills. Gravid females flew over the pastures but could not find their food plants.

You may wonder why the delicate balance of the large blue was dependent upon rabbits, when these animals are not an indigenous species. They were introduced in about the eleventh century. How did the large blue survive before then? The answer must be that there were meadows or clearings where the turf was short — perhaps grazed by deer or where the soil was impoverished — and the thyme was easily accessible.

The number of generations a butterfly has depends on the species. Some, like the orange tip, the Scotch argus (*Erebia aethiops*) and the grayling (*Hipparchia semele*) have one generation only each year. Others like the holly blue, the speckled wood, wall and the common blue (*Polyommatus icarus*) have two each year, and pest species like the large and small white (*Pieris rapae*) have two or more each year. The weather alters the rate at which caterpillars develop. If it is warm they will pass through their instars rather more quickly than if it is dull and cold. This would produce either early or late flights of butterflies.

Caterpillars respond to the short days and chill evenings of the autumn. The last instar caterpillar of the large white butterfly can accurately measure the number of daylight hours per day and can tell the difference between 14½ and 15 hours of light. If there are less than 15 hours each day the caterpillar will turn into a hibernating chrysalis which will not come out until the following spring, perhaps nine months later. If it is more than 15 hours the chrysalis produces a butterfly a week or two later. This intriguing facility of the caterpillar is put to good use in the continuous cultures of butterflies bred in captivity. With the prudent use of artificial light and artificial diets you can create a continuous summer with butterflies hatching regularly through the year.

But how do caterpillars count time so accurately? It seems an incredible feat. It appears that light energy (it comes in small packages called photons) passes through transparent gates in the cuticle of the caterpillar and is absorbed in the body tissues. This is true for the large white. It is suspected that carotenoid pigments may be involved in absorbing light energy.

For European butterflies the commonest way of passing the winter is the caterpillar stage. Most of the browns, fritillaries and blues, coppers and hairstreaks hibernate as caterpillars. There are exceptions though. It is perhaps a facet of the caterpillars' ability to survive cold weather, even down to −14°C, that allows it to withstand such rigours of the climate. Caterpillars do not freeze in winter, they have a natural anti-freeze in their blood. In some species it is a sugar called sorbitol, in others, like the apollos, it is glycerides, which gives protection. The apollo can withstand very cold weather including occasional snowstorms thanks to these glycerides. After cold spells the butterflies sometimes feel rather greasy due to the fat-soluble glycerides. These chemicals are probably also in the tissues of the caterpillar and the chrysalis. Glycerides are said to occur elsewhere in some members of the Lycaenidae. In contrast some aphids have a wax layer to withstand sub-zero temperatures.

In higher latitudes and within the Arctic Circle the short summer season is not sufficiently long for full development of some of the caterpillars of the brown butterflies. Some caterpillars hibernate twice, as in the Arran brown (*Erebia ligea*), the Arctic grayling (*Oeneis bore*), the Arctic woodland ringlet (*Erebia medusa polaris*) and the dewy ringlet (*Erebia pandrose*). Some butterfly species do not necessarily hibernate in the same stage each year; the wall may overwinter as a caterpillar or as a chrysalis and Reverdin's blue (*Lycaeides argyrognomon*) may go into hibernation either as an egg or as a newly hatched caterpillar.

A few butterfly species spend the winter as tiny caterpillars, freshly out of their eggs. The white admiral (*Lagoda camilla*) caterpillar spins a honeysuckle (*Lonicera* spp.) leaf to the stem before leaf-fall (in the middle of November) and rests inside the withered and wrinkled leaf until the spring. It then emerges from its 'hibernaculum' and feeds on the new shoots to continue its development. The caterpillar of the poplar admiral (*Ladoga populi*) constructs a leaf tube which it attaches to a twig as its form of a hibernaculum. The caterpillars of the marbled white and the small skipper eat only their egg cases before going into hibernation for nine months. The caterpillars of the large blue spend the winter in the safer and warmer quarters of particular ant species' galleries whilst they are in their third and fourth instars.

CHRYSALISES

The chrysalis represents the stage between the fully grown caterpillar and the butterfly. Possession of a chrysalis stage by an insect means that it has a complete metamorphosis; each of the four stages — egg, caterpillar, chrysalis and adult — are completely different from each other. This is in direct contrast to insects such as grasshoppers which have an incomplete metamorphosis with no chrysalis stage. Metamorphosis means a change in form and in no other stage is it more obvious than in the chrysalis.

The tough outer case of the chrysalis hides a complex series of biochemical events which transform the caterpillar into a perfectly formed butterfly. If you could see into a chrysalis (if you are gardening you may accidentally damage a moth chrysalis in the soil) you would see that the contents appear just like a yellowish liquid soup. From this will eventually be produced a perfect butterfly, complete in all its sophisticated body systems, hormonal, respiratory, sensory, as well as scales, legs and wings. What happens to this 'soup' is that certain 'organiser' cells seem to rush around and collect other cells round them. Gradually the complex organs of the body take shape and the butterfly is formed.

Butterflies, unlike most moths, do not have underground chrysalises. There are always exceptions; the chrysalis of the grayling occurs just below the surface of the ground. Being above ground during the sedentary chrysalis stage requires them to be carefully camouflaged or have other devices for escaping detection. Hungry birds in mid-winter are persistent searchers. The marbled white and several of the blues like the chalkhill blue and adonis blue (*Lysandra bellargus*) escape bird predation by being in the leaf litter on the surface of the ground. In butterflies with more than one generation the chrysalis stage may last only about nine days duration, in others where overwintering takes place in this stage, it may last about nine months.

Butterfly chrysalises are not able to move from the position chosen by the fully-grown caterpillar. This means that they cannot escape predators and have to rely principally on coloration and shape for concealment. Many are anchored at the tip of the abdomen to the leaf or stem by a silk pad which the caterpillar prepares at the pupation site. This is typical of all of the browns and nymphalids whose chrysalises hang from grass stems.

In several other species, and in addition to the above, another silken device is used for support. This is the silk girdle, seen in the whites, blues, coppers and hairstreaks and swallowtails. The girdle is carefully woven around the thorax of the chrysalis by the caterpillar after it has made the silk base pad. The girdle restricts movement of the chrysalis away from its substrate. Many butterfly chrysalises have limited movement, waggling from side to side and pivoting from the base pad. These rapid movements, are probably used to deter parasitic wasps when they land on them. Most butterfly chrysalises with girdles face upwards so that hatching insects crawl upwards to dry their wings. In the case of the large copper (*Lycaena dispar*) and the black hairstreak the chrysalis can face down.

Another way of escaping detection is to hide away inside a silk cocoon. Butterflies do not go in for thick protective cocoons like some moths, but just a few, like the *Erebia* ringlet butterflies, the Essex skipper and the silver-spotted skipper have chrysalises enclosed in very fragile and poorly constructed cocoons. Although the caterpillars of the red admiral individually draw together the sides of a leaf with silk they do not pupate inside a leaf tent. Those of the white admiral do.

The shape of butterfly chrysalises is extremely variable. Some, like those of the orange tip, are so characteristic that they can be recognised immediately as particular species. Many are cryptically-coloured, both the shape and colour helping to blend in with the background. Some are leaf-like as in the brimstone (*Gonepteryx rhamni*), purple emperor (*Apatura iris*) and white admiral, whilst others like those of the orange tip and wood white (*Leptidea sinapis*) are pointed and elongated resembling twigs and branches. Should predators still find these concealed chrysalises there may be another fail-safe way of avoiding being eaten. The chrysalis of the green hairstreak (*Callophrys rubi*) is said to make a rasping noise which perhaps acts as a deterrent.

The general colour of butterfly chrysalises is brownish-green. Many of the nymphalid species have chrysalises spangled with gold spots and this may well help to distract predators from thinking that there was something worth investigating. The light glittering off these marks may appear like ordinary light and dark areas in leafy branches.

Colours of chrysalises vary within the species and with age. There are many butterflies, like the swallowtail and the large white whose chrysalises may be either green or brown. The background and incident light determines which form will be produced. But it is not as simple as that. The factors controlling colour determination have not been fully established and have kept generations of lepidopterists happy with coloured lights and backgrounds and experiments in shoe-boxes, to test various theories. The experiments have not advanced much since the classic ones of Sir Edward Poulton (1856–1943) at the end of the last century. Colour in butterflies is discussed in Chapter 5.

BUTTERFLIES

The primary function of the butterfly is to mate and lay eggs. It only has to survive to reproduce. A mountain of food has been eaten by the caterpillar — the main eating stage — from which much of the biochemistry of the butterfly has been made. Time is vital to the butterfly. Most fly in the sunshine and have to find their mates quickly. The weather is a limiting factor — though some mountain butterflies do fly in the drizzle — but bad weather can severely affect their chances of courting and mating even in temperate and Mediterranean climates. The lives of butterflies are usually not more than three weeks so there is much activity to pack in. One way of capitalising on only short spells of good weather in the spring is to have males emerging before females, as in the orange tip, Scotch argus and mountain ringlet (*Erebia epiphron*). By the time the females come out a few days later the 'frustrated' males will quickly find them.

Many butterflies are so local in their distribution that they spend the whole of their lives only in a small meadow, never venturing far. These species of butterflies are not migratory and survive year after year in fragile habitats which could easily be threatened by man or environmental conditions. The southern festoon (*Zerynthia polyxena*) is a typical example.

There is another function of other butterflies and this is to colonise new habitats. There is a genetically controlled stimulus to fly to new territories. We call this migration. The direction flown is often predictable; the intensity varies enormously. Large migrations of some species may only be seen once or twice during our lifetime. Migration is good for those species which indulge in it, since it provides more opportunities to the offspring; new habitats are conquered. Offspring will grow up in new areas, hopefully with less competition from others of their kind. Migration is dealt with in Chapter 9.

So reproduction is the main goal of all butterflies and migration is a useful addition to their survival. Most of the regular migrants are fairly hardy butterflies. Hardy is a suitable adjective for migrant butterflies since some of them, like the painted lady, cover up to 1,500 km when they fly from North Africa to Scandinavia. They have large wings and bodies and look altogether much fitter for the job of flying across Europe than, for instance, the fairly sedentary wood white.

Search and find behaviour in butterflies is very common. It may involve patrolling along the edge of a hedge, woodland margin or forest ride and it may result in finding a mate. In some species the butterflies aggregate in special areas — often sheltered warm spots — where butterfly–butterfly interaction within the species are conducive for courtship and mating. Much of the ritual performed by male butterflies is designed to subdue the female into mating. She may appear 'hard to get' and have to be somewhat pacified with pheromones. In Sweden the rock grayling (*Hipparchia alcyone*) butterflies assemble on cliffs and steep slopes at midday prior to an elaborate courtship ritual. Males seek out females and rest close to them during the late morning. Then in groups of six to seven males they fly up the slopes and fly around the females. Repeating this several times they eventually 'intoxicate' the females sufficiently to let off their aphrodisiac pheromones over them. The females having been subdued mating takes place under a rock or in vegetation. In the speckled wood butterfly the beleaguered female appears to be nearly anaesthetised prior to mating. The adult food plant may also serve as a focus for mating, and in the cranberry fritillary (*Boloria aquilonaris*) several dozens of butterflies flock together in areas where marsh cinquefoil (*Potentilla palustris*) grows. Within the Arctic Circle the dusky-winged fritillary (*Clossiana improba*) plays a cat and mouse game at courtship, the male repeatedly flying and crawling after the female, eventually effecting mating on the rocks or on the peaty terrain. The female's abdomen is so swollen with eggs that she almost drags it along the ground as she crawls.

A considerable amount of light-hearted debate has been had since Miriam Rothschild first mentioned that some butterflies — her Hell's Angels — might actually rape other species. In the close confines of greenhouses interactions between several species often evokes unnatural behaviour. The chief culprit is the male monarch who 'is simply a thug', a 'prime example of nature's male chauvinistic pig' who knocks female monarchs down with his 'love-dust' or tries to mate with other closely-related species or unrelated heliconids. Male orange tips in France are quite brutal according to Miriam Rothschild's observations in Normandy. After most of the butterflies have sought roosting sites during the afternoon, at about 16.45, the males check-out the sleeping females, knock them from their sites and assault them remorselessly. Males are given a hard time until they are recognised as males. If the females have already been mated they give the male the 'not-tonight-dear' response with their abdomens fully raised.

Most butterflies need nectar as a vital day-to-day energy source. Nectar is made up of carbohydrates (sugars) which are easily converted into energy. Butterflies find nectar by following the 'honey-guides' on the petals of colourful petals which point to the way of the nectaries. With their uncoiled tongue (proboscis) they suck up the nectar into their alimentary canal for quick digestion. Most butterflies have to find flowers for much of the day and will prodigiously visit flower after flower for hours at a time.

Butterflies live between two weeks and ten months depending on whether they hibernate or not. The average life of a non-hibernating species of butterfly is between two to six weeks, though the precise length is not known in most species. The necessary mark and recapture experiments to verify longevity have not been done so there is plenty of interesting work for observational naturalists. Work done by this writer in marking some 68 specimens of the scarce swallowtail (*Iphiclides podalirius*) in France showed that the longest they lived in the wild was 15 days.

The non-hibernators and non-migrant butterflies like the silver-washed and the dark green fritillary, live about five to six weeks on average. The weather can curtail the length of a butterfly's life, particularly late summer individuals of the red admiral and painted lady in Britain. The onset of a chilly autumn will put an end to any southerly return migration.

In captivity, food is plentiful and predators generally absent, so one might expect the longevity of butterflies to be increased. It has been reliably noted by different workers throughout Europe that the green hairstreak lives up to 45 days, and the swallowtail and the green-veined white both live up to 42 days.

When butterflies die of old age in the wild they do not last long since they have relatively soft bodies and are readily dismembered and eaten by ants. Actually there is a greater chance of their being eaten by predators before they die through natural means but in either case there are usually not many of their remains around for us to see, certainly not enough of them to learn more about their length of life.

Hibernating butterflies live much longer. Their metabolic rate slows down and they are able to live without feeding by gradually using their body fat reserves. Both sexes hibernate and mate in the following spring, though there has been some controversy about females of certain species mating before hibernating in the autumn. The common hibernators in Europe are the small tortoiseshell, large tortoiseshell (*Nymphalis polychloros*), Camberwell Beauty (*Nymphalis antiopa*), the comma, the nettle-tree butterfly (*Libythea celtis*) and the brimstone.

These butterflies have great adaptations for hibernation. They have evolved varying strategies for survival. The comma relies upon the broken up nature of its wing edges and dark undersides for hiding in old leaves and on timbers and the brimstone has an ivy-leaf shape with a green-yellow colour suitable, presumably, for hibernation amongst ivy leaves. A dark underside colour is seen in many species so that when the bright fore wing colours have been tucked away the deception is very effective.

The brimstone is important since it may have been this species which gave butterflies their name. It is butter-coloured and it may have been the first and the last butterfly ever seen each year. In the autumn it is seen fluttering round the banks of ivy and in the spring it is often the first to come out on those warmest days in February and March. Some exceptional specimens may actually live longer than ten months, almost up to a year.

The small tortoiseshell is also a contender for being seen early and late in the season. It is the one which frequently comes indoors in late summer and autumn, apparently seeking hibernation quarters. It may come in quite early on in the summer just when you feel the weather is at its best for butterflies. In fact the nettle-tree butterfly also goes into hibernation early on, really to get away from the dehydrating effect of the summer sun. This escape from adverse summer weather is called aestivation, a form of diapause and can run concurrently with hibernation. In the hotter areas of central Italy, in Tuscany, the meadow brown goes into aestivation for several weeks during the summer.

Where there are two or more generations of butterflies each year it is usually the last generation which hibernates. In the comma, there is a very interesting staggered development of caterpillars through the year in England and also in eastern Sweden; and probably many other places elsewhere in Europe. There are usually two generations of the butterflies each year, but there are some slow developers amongst the caterpillars which only produce one generation of butterflies by the autumn. The rapid developers produce the lighter-coloured form *hutchinsonii* which results in a second generation, though not every year in Sweden. In the spring, related butterflies of the previous year's first and second generation may mate as backcrosses. By doing this the butterflies are perpetuating a useful method of distributing the load of many caterpillars feeding on the same food plant. Other advantages are that predators could not eliminate all the caterpillars or chrysalises at one time and that adverse weather conditions would not necessarily take their toll.

The spring is a good time to see hibernators. They are often relatively

Figure 3.3 Mating pair of marbled whites (life size)

inactive in the chilly air of spring and are not so lively as summer butterflies. You can get closer to them for study and photography. This is particularly true of the Camberwell Beauty which spends much of its time basking in the sun in river valleys or on low branches in southern France. In the summer it is up and away in the top branches of willows and sallows. The author has seen the nettle-tree butterfly aggregating on selected apple trees, before the leaf buds have fully opened — all dibbing away with their tongues at the secretions exuding from the buds. Clearly they were benefiting from some sugary secretion or minerals needed for their hormone system.

A back room, conservatory, garden shed or garage is a good place to find small tortoiseshells and peacocks hibernating. Few people have seen the comma hibernating since it chooses the base of trees and wilted leaves close to the ground in which to seek shelter. Tortoiseshells may get in the folds of the curtains or under the pelmets and are best left alone. They flutter at windows and become active on warm days but the best artificial environment they select is a room which does not have any temperature fluctuation and is relatively cool.

4 Food plants

I'd be a butterfly born in a bower,
Where roses and lilies and violets meet.

Thomas Haynes Bayly (1797–1839) *I'd be a Butterfly*

INTRODUCTION

There is an intimate association between butterflies and plants and their lives are inextricably linked. Wild plants have always co-evolved with insects, fossil evidence proves this. All brightly-coloured flowers are coloured especially for insects. The wind-pollinated flowers do have a colour but it is not bright. This parallel co-evolution (or co-development, co-adaption or mutualism) is a product of thousands of years of evolution. Colourful wild flowers are not pollinated unless they attract and use the services of insects. Insects are unwitting participants in this widespread form of co-evolution and serve a vital role in pollination. Bees and flies are the major pollinators amongst insects. Butterflies and moths are attracted to a huge variety of wild plants but they are not regarded as very important pollinators.

Butterflies visit plants for four important reasons; to drink nectar, to lay their eggs, and to hide away from bad weather or predators and to overwinter on. None of the European butterflies collects and eats pollen from flowers, like the heliconids of South America. This chapter deals just with the caterpillar food plants of butterflies.

The distribution of butterflies is heavily dependent upon the availability of their food plants. Migrants move out of their breeding areas and if they do not find suitable food plant sources in their new localities they will fail to generate a further generation. Often, though, the butterflies are successful in these new localities and establish new populations. Such expansions have been seen in Britain for the orange tip (*Anthocharis cardamines*), and the white admiral (*Ladoga camilla*) and peacock (*Inachis io*).

However, the range of a butterfly can be severely checked if the food plant does not exist beyond a certain region even though the butterfly itself may be able to disperse to other regions. Such is the case with the brimstone (*Gonepteryx rhamni*) whose northerly distribution in England mirrors that of its buckthorn food plants. In fact there are two buckthorn species, alder buckthorn (*Frangula alnus*) and purging buckthorn (*Rhamnus catharticus*) both of which are used as caterpillar food plants. North of the English-Scottish border the food plants are rare and the brimstone is only a casual migrant from the south.

Normally the caterpillar's food plant is the same species for multi-generation butterflies, but the holly blue (*Celastrina argiolus*) is an exception in Europe. The first generation caterpillars feed on holly, the second on ivy. Butterflies emerging from chrysalises in the spring lay their eggs after mating on the flowers of holly. Both male and female flowers, which are on separate trees, are used. It is thought that only the eggs laid on female trees (those that will carry the berries) will survive since the caterpillars require the developing flowers and fruits to live, but recent works shows that caterpillars on male flowers soon go on to nibbling the young soft leaves at the growing point. In some regions neither holly nor ivy is used. Both generations may be on gorse (*Ulex* spp.). Other food plants have been found such as dogwood (*Cornus* spp.), alder (*Alnus* spp.) and snowberry (*Symphoricarpos* spp.). In Scandinavia bog wortleberry (*Vaccinium uliginosum*) and bell heather (*Erica cinerea*) are regularly used. Ivy is not found further north than 60° 32′ N in Norway and is absent from most of the USSR, so the butterfly is bound to have these other food plants.

Quite how egg-laying females find their food plants is a matter of sophisticated chemical detection. Butterflies, such as cabbage whites (*Pieris brassicae*) detect cabbage fields by following upwind the sulphur-rich odours emitted from the plants. They fly low and use this method of olfactory detection very successfully. On your walks in the countryside you will often see a butterfly taking a keen interest in plants, even going inside thickets, bramble clumps or deep down into grass tussocks. They are usually females in search of the very best place to lay their eggs. I have trailed wood whites (*Leptidea sinapis*) for hours in France waiting on their every inspection of plants in the hope that they might stay still for a moment long enough for me to take a photograph. But they go on prospecting for hours. In contrast I have seen the spring lanes of the Burren in western Ireland full of wood whites all stationary on the roadside flowers. Here they were very much more obliging and spent much time feeding from birdsfoot-trefoil (*Lotus corniculatus*).

FOOD PLANTS

Insects may have only a single food plant that their caterpillars will survive on (monophagous), or be limited to just a few species (oligo-phagous), or there may be many species to choose from (polyphagous). Butterflies fall mostly into the first two groups. They never get close to the catholic tastes of certain moth caterpillars like those of the garden tiger (*Arctia caja*) which eats many garden weeds. The most polyphagous are brown butterflies whose caterpillars feed on a variety of grasses.

There are actually very few butterfly species which have single food plant species, although there are several which are limited to one plant genus (see Table 4.1). This is not surprising since plants have speciated just as much as butterflies. Thus one closely related species of the same

Table 4.1 Butterflies and plant genera

i) Butterfly species asociated with one plant genus:

Butterfly		Plant genus	
Apollo	*Parnassius* spp.	*Sedum* spp.	(stonecrops)
Festoons	*Zerynthia* spp.	*Aristolochia* spp.	(birthworts)
Brimstone, Cleopatra	*Gonepteryx* spp.	*Rhamnus* spp.	(buckthorns)
White admirals	*Ladoga* spp.	*Lonicera* spp.	(honeysuckles)
Purple emperor	*Apatura* spp.	*Salix* spp.	(willows, sallow)
Fritillaries (several spp.)	*Argynnis* spp.	*Viola* spp.	(violets)
Duke of Burgundy fritillary	*Hamearis lucina*	*Primula* spp.	(cowslips, primroses)

ii) Butterfly species associated with several plant genera:

Butterfly		Plant genera	
Dingy skipper	*Erynnis tages*	*Lotus, Hippocrepis*	(trefoils, vetches)
Swallowtails	*Papilio* spp.	*Daucus, Ferula, Foeniculum*	(carrot, fennels)
Large white	*Pieris brassicae*	*Brassica, Barbarea*	(crucifers)
Most coppers	*Lycaena* spp.	*Rumex, Polygonum*	(docks)

plant genus is likely to taste similar and be checked out successfully by the same chemical detection system that butterflies employ. All these butterflies could be regarded as having single food plants. Many butterflies fall into the next category of having a few plant genera, sometimes of different plant families, at their disposal as possible food plants, i.e. being oligophagous.

Closely related butterflies can have different food plant preferences within the same plant genus. Whilst the purple emperor (*Apatura iris*) feeds on sallow (*Salix cinerea*), the lesser purple emperor (*Apatura ilia*) is found on poplar (*Populus* spp.); both plants belong to the willow family (Salicaceae).

The swallowtails of the genus *Papilio* are an interesting group since they have co-evolved with members of one single plant family, the Umbelliferae. The Corsican swallowtail (*P. hospiton*) uses the impressive giant fennel (*Ferula communis*), whilst the Continental swallowtails (*P. machaon*) often feed on ordinary fennel (*Foeniculum vulgare*). In Britain the same swallowtail feeds exclusively on milk parsley (*Peucedanum palustre*) whereas its Continental cousins will also feed on wild carrot (*Daucus carota*). In Sweden Christer Wiklund's important research showed that the two major food plants are milk parsley and angelica (*Angelica archangelica*). Alexanor (*P. alexanor*) feeds on yet other umbellifers, *Sesili*, *Trinia* and *Tychotis* genera.

The scarce swallowtail (*Iphiclides podalirius*) is an exception which departs from the Umbelliferae family since it has co-evolved with woody plant species. Hawthorn (*Crataegus* spp.), sloe (*Prunus spinosa*) and cherry (*Prunus* spp.) figure strongly amongst its diet. These happen to be the identical food plants of the caterpillars of the black-veined white (*Aporia crataegi*). The two butterfly species are from different families but they often live in the same habitats in Europe.

The apollo butterflies of mountainous regions in Europe have co-evolved with several different plant genera some of which are well represented at higher altitude. *P. apollo* feeds on the large group of stonecrops (*Sedum* spp.), the small apollo (*P. phoebe*) feeds on yellow saxifrage (*Saxifraga aizoides*) as well as houseleek (*Sempervivum montanum*) and the clouded apollo (*P. mnemosyne*) feeds on corydalis (*Corydalis* spp.). These plants belong to two closely related plant families, the Crassulaceae and the Saxifragaceae.

Butterflies and Elms

In a wild habitat quite unaffected by man the dependence of a butterfly species upon a single species of food plant must be regarded as perfectly successful. But habitats always change by natural means and fluctuations in butterfly populations, possibly extinctions, may occur. The best example is the demise of the elm trees in western Europe. In Britain alone since 1960 over 20 million trees have died owing to Dutch Elm disease — a fungus carried by specific bark beetles. The disease is still continuing unabated today on the Continent.

There are two important native species of elm in Europe. The wych elm (*Ulmus glabra*) and the common elm (*Ulmus procera*, called the English elm in Britain). Hybrids have been formed between these two species and there are several other introduced ornamental elm species. Elms typically reproduce by suckering and it used to be a typical scene to see, before

Dutch Elm disease took hold, clones of offspring from the parent tree adjacent to each other in decreasing height along the hedgerow. Most of the dead elms in the countryside were the common elm many of which had been planted in the eighteenth century. Suckers may be exceedingly common today along hedgerows, but when mature, the sapling trees quickly succumb to the disease. For the first few years the elm-rich hedgerows can support a useful breeding colony of butterflies, but when their bark becomes thick the beetles soon move in.

But what effect has the decline in elms had on British butterflies? It was traditionally said that the white-letter hairstreak (*Strymonidia w-album*) had a preference for wych elm. This would seem logical, if true, since wych elm slightly predates the common oak in its ancestry. Thanks to Sir Richard Southwood's theory we now know that the older a tree is in evolutionary terms the more insects there are associated with it; thus it is likely that the butterfly started its evolutionary life on this older tree species.

None of the three species of European butterflies associated with the elm is exclusively dependent upon it (see Table 4.2). Alternative food plants are available. The large tortoiseshell (*Nymphalis polychloros*) may have been heavily reliant upon elms since its numbers in Britain have declined drastically in the last 30 years to such an extent that most people never see it today. According to John Heath 'it was last recorded in any abundance before 1948'. However, Professor E.B. Ford noted that the decline had occurred much earlier and it was not uncommon in southern England up to about 1903, when it suddenly became rare. In other parts, up to the 1920s, it was quite frequent. The large tortoiseshell may survive on its other food plants such as willows, poplars, aspen, whitebeam, birch, cherry though it is now fairly infrequent in Europe. Clearly some factor other than the demise of the elms was responsible. Other theories put forward recently blame heavy parasitism — up to 99 per cent of caterpillars may be parasitised by the ichneumonid *Apanteles glomeratus* — or there may have been just a long-term fluctuation in the population. Both this species and the white-letter hairstreak were well known to have strong breeding colonies established on single mature elm trees. Many authors talked about the special 'favourite' trees of butterflies but lots of them have now vanished, taking with them many flourishing butterfly populations.

The Cabbage Feeders

Another group of the oligophagous butterflies are the whites which show a distinct preference for the cabbage family. The large white is regarded as an oligophagous species yet it has been accredited with no less than 83 food plants, most belonging to the cabbage family (Cruciferae). Its caterpillars are rather partial to the Tropaeolaceae as well. Most of the food plants are crucifers since they contain the necessary volatile chemicals (mustard oil glycosides) which attract egg-laying females.

The two menacing species in the kitchen garden are the small white (*Pieris rapae*) and the large white. Even though the caterpillars of both species may be trying to eat the same plant there is often no competition between them, unless food is limited. The caterpillars of the large white are brightly-coloured and feed exposed on the outer leaves of the plant; those of the small white feed discreetly in the heart of the cabbage. These are the ones which happen to turn up on the plate, their cryptic colours

Figure 4.1   A menace in the kitchen garden is the female large white

defying detection. Their background matching colours are ideal for life on green leaves.

The green-veined white (*Artogeia napi*) differs from these two by having no connection with the crops of the kitchen garden. In fact in 1974 it was recommended by Otakar Kudrna that the green-veined white should be removed from the *Pieris* genus and set apart in its own *Artogeia* genus. It is a butterfly of damp meadows, ditches and waysides where it lays its eggs on wild members of the cabbage family; species like lady's smock (*Cardamine pratensis*) and mignonette (*Reseda* spp.) and mustards (*Sisymbrium* spp.). The only time that a green-veined white might venture into a kitchen garden would be to visit the tall flowers of radishes, or their like gone to seed. Several other species of the whites have co-evolved with members of the Cruciferae as their staple food plants such as the Bath white (*Pontia daplidice*) and most of the orange tips.

Co-evolution with a major plant family which is widely represented in Europe is one of the keys to the success of the whites. This is of paramount importance to the migrant butterflies such as the large and small whites. With many hundreds of species of crucifers in Europe they have found suitable species for support in all of the regions they have exploited. They are therefore able to maintain large populations over a very wide area and can reinforce populations that fail locally.

The Nettle Feeders

The selection of nettles (*Urtica* spp.) as food plants was a very successful evolutionary strategy. There are few species of nettles (common, small and Roman) but they are mostly very successful and widespread in Europe. The advantages to migrants are again obvious. Another ecological advantage is that selective-grazing animals tend to leave stands of nettle alone because of their stinging hairs. The gregarious caterpillars of the nettle feeders are then left alone by many predators but still have the onslaughts of parasitic wasps with which to contend.

Several of the nymphalid butterflies lay their eggs on nettles. Perhaps the most well known are those of the small tortoiseshell (*Aglais urticae*) and the peacock whose gregarious caterpillars are familiar sights in gardens. The red admiral (*Vanessa atalanta*) caterpillars also feed on nettle but their caterpillars are solitary and less frequently seen. Another butterfly which exploits nettles is the map butterfly (*Arachnia levana*).

The southern comma (*Polygonia egea*) also exploits the nettle family since its caterpillars feed on pellitory-of-the-wall (*Parietaria* spp.). This is a very widespread plant often seen on old walls and masonry of churches and castles. Closely related to the nettles is the cannabis family (Cannabiaceae) which has as its only native species in Europe — the hop (*Humulus lupulus*). The comma (*Polygonia c-album*) also uses the hop as one of the principal food plants though it will use gooseberry (*Grossularia uva-crispa*) in the garden.

The painted lady (*Cynthia cardui*) uses thistles (*Cirsium* spp. Compositae) as its principal food plant — another plant which is prickly to grazers (except goats which eat them with impunity), but it will occasionally be found on nettles. Like nettles, the thistles are armed with deterrents for grazers.

Many of the nymphalid butterflies are found in association with man. The reason is fairly clear to see. Nettles thrive on ground disturbed by man, often enriched with nitrogenous waste, and indeed nettles are indicators of nitrogen-rich soils. This is one of the reasons why species like the small tortoiseshell are so common in urban areas and gardens.

The Grass Feeders

Two families of butterflies have exploited rich grassland reserves. These are the skippers and the browns. If ever there was a highly successful group of plants, which grows through most of the year and is present almost everywhere, the grasses fit the bill. The skippers and browns have exploited them thoroughly.

One could make some tentative suggestions regarding the future of these two butterfly families. As their food plants are available and widespread throughout the year one might expect the butterflies to be very common. This is certainly the case with the meadow brown (*Maniola jurtina*), the small skipper (*Thymelicus sylvestris*), the small heath (*Coenonympha pamphilus*) and to a lesser extent the Essex skipper (*Thymelicus lineola*). But there are butterflies like the chequered skipper (*Carterocephalus palaemon*) which are very severely restricted in distribution in Britain.

The marbled whites (*Melanargia* spp.) and the ringlet (*Aphantopus hyperantus*) which broadcast their eggs over grass areas can be very common. Counts of 60-odd marbled whites along a short piece of grassy track on chalk are not uncommon. Wet meadows full of ringlets and ditches full of small heaths in the autumn are still found in some rural areas.

Surprisingly the precise species of grasses used by many of the commoner browns is still either unknown or conjectural. There is a suggestion that for the meadow brown at least the type of grass species is not very important. In the latest assessment of the state of British butterflies Ernest Pollard says of the hedge brown there is 'little reliable information on any preferences'; and that 'like most grass-feeding butterflies, it is not entirely clear which species are used in the wild'; or of the speckled wood (*Pararge aegeria*) 'the relative importance of the many species [of grass] used is not known'. It is surprising that, after 400 years of amateur and professional butterfly-hunting, these basic queries still remain.

Figure 4.2 The large heath is a typical grassland butterfly

The wild moorland of Scotland or the extensive *tourbières* (bogs) and *causses* (limestone plateaux) of Europe are ideal places for many of the browns and skippers. The grayling (*Hipparchia semele*) is one species which is found in several different habitats and in each may exploit completely different species of grass. In sand dunes it has been seen to lay its eggs on marram grass (*Ammophila arenaria*), on bristle bent (*Agrotis setaceae*) on acid soil and sheep's fescue (*Festuca ovina*) on chalky soils.

Equally at home on grassy motorway embankments, green *aires* (rest areas) on the French autoroutes or ordinary roadside verges both the small and Essex skippers are keen exploiters of coarse grasses growing in any recently disturbed areas. Meadow browns and small heaths may also be very common on waste land and wild corners of parks, gardens and golf courses in suburbia.

A rare grass-feeding skipper is the chequered skipper. The demise of the chequered skipper from English localities in 1975 caught entomologists by surprise. At present the butterfly survives in western Scotland, even along an 8 km stretch of roadside verge. This demonstrates that some butterflies are quick to colonise brand new habitats created by man. Clearly 'ancient' habitats are not required by this butterfly species. The caterpillars have been found on brome (*Bromus* spp.), false brome (*Brachypodium sylvaticum*) and tor-grass (*B. pinnatum*) but more research is needed on its other possible food plants.

The Violet Feeders

The fritillaries deserve special attention not only because of their beauty but because of their affinities with violets. Any entomologist who ventures into Europe will be immediately surprised at how many similar-looking fritillaries there are. They are painfully difficult to identify in the wild and the only reliable method is to catch them and look at their patterns and colours. Even then identification may be difficult. Unfortunately many have to be killed for thorough analysis.

All this is evidence that great speciation has occurred within this group. They exhibit adaptive radiation, which means that different species have exploited many different habitats. During the summer months lowland meadows and roadsides are full of a great variety of fritillaries and it is possible to see up to ten different species in one place during the day. The individual variation which they exhibit also plays havoc with identification.

Many of the fritillary species in Europe have co-evolved with violets as their staple caterpillar food plant. But there are exceptions. The heath fritillary (*Mellicta athalia*) has evolved with plantains (*Plantago* spp.) and cow-wheats (*Melampyrum* spp.); the marbled fritillary (*Brenthis daphne*) with bramble (*Rubus* spp.); and the scarce fritillary (*Hypodryas maturna*) has evolved with tree species, ash (*Fraxinus* spp.) and poplar (*Populus* spp.). There are also many fritillary species for which we are still ignorant about the food plants. A number of the butterfly species listed in Higgins and Riley's *Butterflies of Britain and Europe* as having unknown food plants, are given food plant sources or possible ones by Henriksen and Kreutzer. The Arctic fritillary (*Clossiana chariclea*) uses perhaps the Lapland cassiope (*Cassiope tetragore*) or violets, the dusky-winged fritillary (*Glossiana improba*) uses *Polygonum viviparum*, and the Lapland fritillary (*Hypodryas iduna*) has co-evolved with plantains and speedwells (*Veronica alpina* and *V. fruticans*). There still remains the Asian fritillary (*Hypodryas intermedia*), the Balkan fritillary (*Boloria graeca*) and the little fritillary (*Mellicta asteria*) for which we do not know the food plants.

At least a dozen fritillary species have violets as their food plants. Like many other species which depend upon one genus of plants for survival their future is therefore not guaranteed. Violets grow in the shade of young woodlands, around the margins of mature woodlands, in coppice woods and along wayside banks. Many of these habitats have been eliminated by man with 'improvement' of land, often involving the complete grubbing out of woods. Though violets are prolific seed producers they have not been able to re-establish populations. The dependent butterflies have unfortunately declined and disappeared with them.

The names of violet are frequently confused but the following are eaten by European fritillary species: long-spurred *V. calcarata*, hairy *V. hirta*, pale dog *V. lactaea*, marsh *V. palustris*, early dog *V. reichenbachiana*, dog *V. riviniana* and wild pansy or heartsease *V. tricolor*.

It is not clear at all which species of violets each particular species of fritillary feeds on, though the species listed above have all had fritillary caterpillars feeding on them at some time. The most important issue of this association is that these fritillaries have become so intimately co-evolved with the *Viola* genus. Species like *Fabriciana elisa*, *F. niobe*, *Clossiana titania*, *C. dia* and *C. thore* are often mentioned in books as just 'violets'. The violet species is probably not very important since the active chemical principles which make violets what they are, are probably widely distributed in several species.

In Britain there appears to be a regional preference in violet species with the pearl-bordered fritillary (*Boloria euphrosyne*). It feeds on *V. riviniana* in the south and *V. palustris* in the north. Both the small pearl-bordered fritillary (*Boloria selene*) and the Queen of Spain (*Issoria lathonia*) feed on *V. riviniana*.

The Plantain and Cow-wheat Feeders

Some of the fritillaries have co-evolved with the Scrophulariaceae plant family. Cow-wheats, toadflaxes (*Linaria* spp.) and speedwells (*Veronica* spp.) all belong to this family and are used by some butterfly species. Plantains are used by several species as alternatives with cow-wheat as in Nickerl's (*Mellicta aurelia*), heath (*Mellicta athalia*) and false heath (*Melitaea diamina*) fritillaries.

It is not surprising to find the spotted fritillary (*Melitaea didyma*) using either plantain or toadflax (*Linaria*) as they both belong to the same family. Or to find the heath fritillary using germander speedwell (*Veronica chamaedryas*) as a 'starter' food source in south-west England and cow-wheat in the east since they are all members of the Scrophulariaceae. The heath fritillary also uses ribwort plantain (*Plantago lanceolata*) as its major food source in south-west England. This is also the food plant of the Glanville fritillary (*Melitaea cinxia*). The marsh fritillary (*Euphydryas aurinia*) feeds on devil's-bit scabious (*Succisa pratensis*) as its main food plant, but also on plantain.

Alpine Flowers

Another interesting facet of the fritillaries is their association with alpine flowers. This has, therefore, given them the ability to exploit the high alpine meadows, pastures, plateaux and *causses*, where the climatic conditions are more rigorous. Often inhospitable countryside which has

Figure 4.3   Cow-wheat, the major food plant of the heath fritillary in Britain

Table 4.2 Alpine flowers as butterfly food plants
(Botanists generally regard alpine species as those growing above 1,000 m)

Common plant name	Scientific plant name	Common butterfly name	Scientific butterfly name
Polygonaceae (dock family)			
Alpine bistort	*Polygonum viviparum*	Mountain fritillary	*Boloria napaea*
Crassulaceae (stonecrop family)			
Stonecrop	*Sedum* spp.	Apollo butterflies	*Parnassius* spp.
		Chequered blue	*Scolitantides orion*
Rosaceae (rose family)			
Cloudberry	*Rubus chamaemorus*	Freija's fritillary	*Clossiana frigga*
Mountain avens	*Dryas octopetala*	Polar fritillary	*Clossiana polaris*
Lady's mantles	*Alchemilla* spp.	Cynthia's fritillary	*Hypodryas intermedia*
Papilionaceae (pea and vetch family)			
Alpine milk vetch	*Astragalus alpinus*	Alpine argus	*Abulina orbitulus*
Primulaceae (primrose family)			
Alpine snowbell	*Soldanella alpina*	Glandon blue	*Agriades glandon*
Ericaceae (heather family)			
Cranberry	*Vaccinium oxycoccus*	Cranberry fritillary	*Boloria aquilonaris*
		Cranberry blue	*Vaccinina optilete*
Cassiope	*Cassiope tetragore*	Polar fritillary	*Clossiana polaris*
Gentianaceae (gentian family)			
Gentians	*Gentiana* spp.	Grison's fritillary	*Mellicta varia*
Scrophulariaceae (figwort family)			
Alpine speedwell	*Veronica alpina*	Lapland fritillary	*Euphydras iduna*

late frosts (up to early August), high winds, sparse plants, little cover, cool summers and severe winter conditions are colonised successfully and efficiently by these butterflies. Butterflies from other families have moved into these areas too. As well as fritillaries there are blues, browns and skippers found there.

The species listed in Table 4.2 are not exhaustive but give a good idea of the range of species of butterfly and the alpine flowers utilised. There are some familiar alpine plants such as the gentians which are the exclusive food plants of some butterflies, but several of the butterfly species have alternative food sources. Walkers in the Alps, Pyrénées, Massif Central of France and in Scandinavia will have seen the tracksides full of thistles, knapweeds and scabious. Here the Freyer's fritillary (*Melitaea arduinna*) and the knapweed fritillary (*Melitaea phoebe*) live as caterpillars on the knapweeds (*Centaurea* spp.). On calcareous soils the tall biennial mulleins (e.g. *Verbascum thapsus*) may support caterpillars of the lesser-spotted fritillary (*Melitaea trivia*). The silver-spotted skippers (*Hesperia comma*) still struggle in the high winds and grassy expanses to find their food plants such as the tussock grasses. The boreo-alpine species like the dewy ringlet (*Erebia pandrose*) uses alpine grasses and the alpine grizzled skipper (*Pyrgus andromedae*) still has an unknown food plant. These species live in the sub-Arctic lowlands and the south European mountains and are absent from the intervening lowlands. They were much more widely distributed but retreated to the colder northern regions or up mountains after the last Ice Age.

Much of the mountainous Mediterranean countryside is covered with rock roses (*Helianthemum* spp.) forming a spectacular display of white and pink colours in the spring and summer. There are many species of rock rose and they are the food plants of the brown argus (*Aricia agestis*), a lowland species and its relation, the northern brown argus (*Aricia artaxerxes*) which is a boreo-alpine species. The geranium and storksbills (*Geranium* spp.) which are typical of stony and waste areas are also used by the geranium argus (*Eumedonia eumedon*) and the silvery argus (*Aricia nicias*).

The Vetch Feeders

Two butterfly families have exploited the pea family (Papilionaceae) of clovers, medicks, vetches and trefoils. These are the Pieridae and the Lycaenidae. The pierids are normally associated with the cabbage (Cruciferae) family through the notorious depredations of the 'cabbage whites', but the clouded yellows (*Colias* spp.) and the wood white (*Leptidea sinapis*) are firmly co-evolved with the pea family. Many of the members of the Papilionaceae live on light sandy soils and chalky areas. This is why many of the blue butterflies are associated with chalk and limestone areas, *causses* and heathlands.

In the Lycaenidae it is predominantly the blues which have co-evolved so extensively with the Papilionidae, using annual, perennial, woody and non-woody plants as food plants. They have not stopped there since there are a few which utilise the Primulaceae, the Umbelliferae and the Labiateae. The close relatives of the blues, the hairstreaks, have mostly co-evolved with tree species such as hawthorn (*Crataegus* spp.), ash, oak (*Quercus* spp.) and elm. The coppers are co-evolved with the docks (*Rumex* spp.) which belong to the Polygonaceae plant family.

The chalkhill blue (*Lysandra coridon*) typifies a species which has a chalk-loving (calcicole) plant as its food plant, the horeseshoe vetch (*Hippocrepis comosa*). This is also used by Berger's clouded yellow (*Colias australis*). Gorse (*Ulex europaeus*) and broom (*Sarothamnus scoparius*) make up an integral part of heathlands and support a number of butterflies between them, such as the green underside blue (*Glaucopsyche alexis*) the silver-studded blue (*Plebejus argus*), and the Danube clouded yellow (*Colias myrmidone*). In many parts of western Europe the green hairstreak's food plant include the Papilionaceae, but in Scotland it feeds on bilberry (*Vaccinium myrtillus*) which is a member of the heather family (Ericaceae). Caterpillars have also been recorded on heather (*Calluna vulgaris*) and bell heather (*Erica cinerea*). The same situation may also occur in western Ireland where the author has seen great numbers of this butterfly in the vast boggy wastes of Connemara National Park.

Vetches such as the Mediterranean crown vetch (*Coronilla varia*) support the Provencal short-tailed blue (*Everes alcetas*) and Reverdin's blue (*Lycaeides argyrognomon*). Crown vetch is typically Mediterranean. The milk vetch (*Astragalus* spp.) supports the zephyr blue (*Plebejus pylaon*), the Cretan argus (*Kretania psylorita*) and the alpine argus (*Abulina orbitulus*).

Sainfoin (*Onobrychis vicifolia*) is now grown more widely in the Mediterranean area as a forage crop. Cottage farmers grow small plots of this attractive plant and, like lucerne (*Medicago sativa*), it is an ideal place to watch and photograph butterflies of many species since they are attracted to the delicate pink flowers and prolific amounts of nectar. The osiris blue (*Cupido osiris*), the damon blue (*Agriodiatus damon*), the furry blue (*A. dolus*) and the eastern wood white (*Leptidea duponcheli*) all lay their eggs on it. The other two wood whites in Europe (*L. sinapis* and *morsei*) use *Lathyrus* species of pea or birdsfoot-trefoil in the case of *L. sinapis*.

The medicks (*Medicago* spp.), to which lucerne belongs, are attractive as caterpillar food plants too. They are the food plants for the African grass jewel (*Zizeeria knysna*) found in Spain and Portugal as well as the short-tailed blue (*Everes argiades*) and the eastern short-tailed blue (*Everes decoloratus*).

One of the reasons for the success of the clouded yellow (*Colias croceus*) in Europe is because it will feed on a wide variety of papilionaceous plants, such as clovers (*Trifolium* spp.), trefoils and lucerne. The pale clouded yellow (*C. hyale*) feeds on clovers, the Greek clouded yellow (*C. libanotica*) on milk vetch and the lesser clouded yellow (*C. chrysotheme*) on hairy tare (*Vicia hirsuta*).

Other Southern European Food Plants

Many typical Mediterranean plants have made their way northwards — dispersed by natural means or introduced by man — and are now quite widespread through western Europe. Indeed, about 30 per cent of the British flora has been introduced, many of the aliens originating from the Mediterranean. But there are several plant species which are highly typical of the Mediterranean and are not found out of this area. Various butterflies have co-evolved with these species.

Lepidopterists in southern Europe never cease to be amazed by the impressive two-tailed pasha (*Charaxes jasius*). Whether it comes down to take sweat from your skin, or is basking on rocks, or is making regular swift passes through the trees, it is a spectacular butterfly with its four 'tails'. Its caterpillar food plant is the strawberry tree (*Arbutus unedo*) which is native to the Mediterranean region and islands. The butterfly — which is the only example of this large nymphalid group of African butterflies in southern Europe — is unknown in northern Europe since the strawberry tree only grows there as an ornamental tree in parks and gardens.

There is a much smaller butterfly species which uses strawberry trees as a food plant, and this is the Chapman's green hairstreak (*Callophrys avis*). In contrast the commoner green hairstreak (*C. rubi*) lays its eggs on members of the Papilionaceae such as gorse and broom. This situation of a large and small unrelated species of butterfly dependent upon one forest tree species recalls the large tortoiseshell and the white-letter hairstreak on elm.

Another butterfly of the Mediterranean which has a typical Mediterranean plant host is the nettle tree butterfly (*Libythea celtis*) which is named after its food plant, the nettle tree (*Celtis australis*). Nettle trees grow tall like other forest trees such as limes (*Tilia* spp.) and have a toothed leaf margin which gives them their name. It is fortunate that nettle trees are often planted in towns and cities in parks, along roads and in market place situations, providing ample food plants for populations of these interesting butterflies. The butterfly is the only member of the 'snout' butterfly family in Europe, it being better represented in the New World.

A familiar plant of waysides and rough areas in the Mediterranean is the heliotrope (*Helioptropium europaeum*) — not to be confused with the winter heliotrope (*Petasites fragrans*) which is also Mediterranean and a widespread road-margin pest in northern Europe. In places it is a pest plant and it is not surprising that butterflies have evolved with this abundant plant. In Greece, Crete and Turkey the grass jewel (*Freyeria trochylus*) uses this as its food plant and, like several other members of the blue family, the caterpillars are thought to be attended by ants.

An attractive roadside tree or bush of small stature is the Christ's thorn (*Paliurus spina-christi*). In early summer its stems are covered with a blaze of distinctive yellow flowers mixed in with the thorny stems which give it its name. It is the food plant of the caterpillars of the little tiger blue (*Tarucus balkanicus*) which is found in the eastern Mediterranean. The distribution of the butterfly is not clear and it may well turn up in the western Mediterranean where its food plant is also found. Another Mediterranean plant species, the jujube bush (*Ziziphus vulgaris*), is food plant for the caterpillars of a related butterfly, the common tiger blue (*Tarucus theophrastus*) which is found in southern Spain. The Mediterranean crown vetch, as mentioned earlier, is used by at least two members of the blue family. Another pea species, the bladder senna (*Colutea arborescens*) is the food plant of the long-tailed blue (*Lampides boeticus*) as well as the iolas blue (*Iolana iolas*).

5 Coloration and camouflage

In the oak woods, in the fen lands,
In the melancholy marshes,
The copper, *Hippothoe*, sang them,
And the Swallowtail, *Machaon*,
And the Emperor, the Iris,
Clad in robes of Tyrian purple.

Edward Newman (1857) *The Insect Hunters*

Butterflies are the most amazingly coloured insects in the world. Their variety of colour even exceeds the gaudily coloured beetles, dragonflies and flies. They range from the brilliant 'metallic' colours of the blues and coppers to the subtle shades of the browns and skippers. A host of intriguing questions always arise with any study of insect colour. Why are there so many different colours and patterns? What are the colouring materials and for whom are the colours designed? This chapter provides some of the answers.

Like many other groups of insects, butterflies are not alone in having diversified into thousands of different species. This natural phenomenon, called adaptive radiation, has resulted in at least 150,000 species of butterfly worldwide. Each has a distinct role (niche) in each of the environments in which it lives. The colours of butterflies are part of the way this speciation has manifested itself in the wild. We can often explain biochemically the nature of insect colour but are not always clear about the reason for selection. The great variety in colour of butterflies continues to intrigue scientists and makes us realise that we are just onlookers of a complex evolutionary system. There is, however, every good reason to suppose that the earliest butterflies, perhaps over 50 million years ago, had colourful wings and could see colour.

Variation is a natural phenomenon; the basis of Charles Darwin's theory of natural selection. All biological features exhibit variation and this includes coloration. Colours and patterns are just one of thousands of characteristics which are passed between generations as part of their gene complex. For an individual it is advantageous to have a wide range of colour forms since one of them may be useful for unforeseen constraints in the environment. It is the small, often undetected, mutations, not the large and obvious ones, which are used by animals for evolution. Some subtle changes in colour hues may prove to be useful for an individual which would live to pass these characteristics on in its genes. Within a few generations distinct colour changes may result as witnessed in the numerous moth species which produced black melanic forms in the process of industrial melanism.

Sometimes there are errors in the biochemical pathways which determine colour; the result is often a freak or 'sport'. These express themselves as albinos, dark forms (melanics) or complete or partial gynandromorphs (part male, part female) with the different colours and patterns of both sexes showing. These extreme forms would normally disappear in the wild and selection would not take place through them. Interesting variants have been assiduously collected over the years and frequently change hands at high prices. The scholarly work of Russwurm's *Aberrations of British Butterflies* (1978) focused attention on this particular study of butterflies.

WARNING COLOURS

The bright colours of butterflies are not necessarily just for individual recognition or deception of predators by evolving colours of poisonous species (mimicry). Many are a form of advertisement. They draw attention purposely to the butterfly. Brightly-coloured butterflies loaded with deterrent poisons are known as having aposematic colours. They provide the 'models' for the palatable 'mimics'.

This has given rise to two strategies of survival. Those that 'want to be seen' and those that do not, anthromorphically speaking. Those that advertise themselves wish to draw attention to themselves, with their bright red, orange, white and black colours. They are generally toxic and rely on the learned behaviour of predators. Predators associate a particular bright colour scheme, say red/black, white/black, yellow/black, with a bad experience when they sampled one of these distasteful insects originally. Butterflies rely on the learned behaviour of birds. The distinctive colours may be arranged as patterns of bands, spots or whole areas like abdomens covered in bright colour. Those that 'do not want to be seen' are generally edible species and it is in their interest to remain undetected and camouflaged. Sometimes brightly-coloured butterflies are also edible and, in this case, may be a mimic.

Insectivorous birds, mammals, and reptiles such as lizards and geckos, have helped to produce the aposematic colours and patterns of warningly-coloured butterflies. They have been the active constraints (or external biotic factors) acting on butterflies and exerting their selective pressures. Colours and patterns which startled or deterred by advertisement became successful. Those caterpillars and butterflies which happened to enrich their bodies with nauseous chemicals from the caterpillar food plants, without killing themselves, were left uneaten and survived to breed. Their offspring were then endowed genetically with the characteristic of being able to store poisons and improved the deterrent system by natural selection. Gradually the relative toxicity built up so that there are now butterflies (and many more moth examples) which are like flying chemistry laboratories loaded with deadly poisons.

The types of poisons found in Lepidoptera are many and varied. Many families of butterflies have evolved this strategy of chemical defence independently on different food plants and rely on completely different poisons. The best examples are the whites (*Pieris* spp.) which have mustard oil glycosides and the rare American visitor, the monarch (*Danaus plexippus*), which has cardiac glycosides in its body. The mustard oil glycosides are the sulphur-rich compounds in cabbage leaves and are responsible for that characteristic cabbage smell when it is cooked. They are not poisonous to humans but are successful deterrents in the caterpillars against birds and lizards. The monarch caterpillars get their supply of toxins from the poisonous milkweed (*Asclepias* spp.) food plant, which is rare in Europe in the wild.

Brightly-coloured butterflies are not always toxic as Miriam Rothschild showed in her feeding experiments. When tits (*Parus* spp.) and field voles (*Microtus agrestis*) tried out red admirals (*Vanessa atalanta*) they ate them eagerly. But what is eaten by one species may be rejected by others. For instance both these predators eat small white butterflies (*Pieris rapae*) but the long-eared bat (*Plecotus auritus*) rejects them. Not that the bat or butterfly are likely to meet each other (though the red admiral is one of the few butterflies known, very occasionally, to fly at night!) but the bat has a discerning palate.

Moths, being far more diverse in species, tend to have an equal array of deterrent poisons as butterflies. In any case the day-flying moths, like the cinnabar moth (*Tyria jacobeae*) and the burnet moth (*Zygaena* spp.) which are dressed in butterfly colours, and the exposed caterpillars of the spurge hawk-moth (*Hyles euphorbiae*) and tiger moths (Arctiidae) are very rich in toxins, such as alkaloids, cardenolides and acetylocholine and histamine.

It always seems remarkable that insects can tolerate highly toxic chemicals in their bodies without being killed by them. We like to feel that they can store away the deterrent poisons in different parts of the body where they take no part in the physiology of the insect, in a grand process of 'compartmentalisation'. A good deterrent system must be backed up with an effective poison. One of the most poisonous is hydrocyanic acid which is found in birdsfoot-trefoil (*Lotus corniculatus*). This is the food plant of the burnet moths which contain this cyanide acid. It is also the food plant of the common blue (*Polyommatus icarus*) and the wood white (*Leptidea sinapis*) butterflies but these have not been investigated for this poisonous deterrent.

Birdsfoot-trefoil occurs in two chemically-different forms. One which does not contain hydrocyanic acid (acyanogenic) and the other which does (cyanogenic). It seems that the plants contain these chemicals as a defence against grazing animals such as sheep, snails and caterpillars, though there are other factors involved. A lot of work on these forms has been carried out on the island of Anglesey off the north Wales coast.

Work done by Miriam Rothschild and her son Charles Lane in the 1960s indicated that the common blue lays its eggs on both strains and that the caterpillars eat both types 'apparently indiscriminately'. The caterpillars contain an enzyme called rhodanese which breaks down these toxins and gives them partial protection to feed on these poisonous plants.

Very many brightly-coloured butterflies are neither aposematic nor mimetic. Their colours serve to make them recognisable to members of their own species, and so promote male–female encounters which lead to mating. Many of these have dull undersides, so that they are concealed with wings closed and conspicuous (and alert) when the wings are opened. The comma (*Polygonia c-album*) is the best example but it is also seen in the red admiral and the small tortoiseshell (*Aglais urticae*).

Green and Yellow Colours

As caterpillars spend much of their lives eating green plant material it is not surprising that some plant pigments are incorporated into their tissues and passed on to the butterfly via the chrysalis. Green leaves and flowers contain all sorts of pigments and chemicals, some of which are used by butterflies for coloration. An oak leaf may contain over 200 different compounds.

In the plant, greens are produced from chlorophylls, yellows, oranges and reds from carotenoids and flavones. The familiar autumn tints are produced from a set of other pigments called anthocyanins which are not used as far as is known in caterpillar or butterfly colours. There is another group of plant pigments called tannins. These are the dark pigments which we enjoy so much in tea. They build up in the autumn and serve as a plant feeding deterrent against leaf-eating insects.

The green chlorophyll pigments are presumed by many to be the most likely candidate for colouring caterpillars green. However they are rarely used as insect pigments since most are broken down soon after eating. In young caterpillars the recently eaten food can sometimes be seen through the transparent cuticle and gives the caterpillar a green colour. The greens that are commonly found in caterpillars are produced in the same way that an artist would make green from mixing yellow and blue. This is called the Tyndall effect. The yellow and orange pigments come direct from the plant and are carotenoids; the blue pigments are the bile pigments used in digestion. They are made by the caterpillar from raw materials.

In nature, green-coloured butterflies are not very common and in Europe there are more green moths like the emeralds (*Geometra* spp.) than butterflies. However, the green hairstreak (*Callophrys rubi*) is unique amongst European butterflies with its distinctive underside green coloration. The green is produced by a different method than mixing pigments. It is made by a structural method — that is the microscopic corrugations on the surface of the scales diffract light and appear green. If a little fat soluble liquid, like ether, is put on the wings the colour vanishes — the liquid filling the gulleys and stopping the diffraction of light. In the green-veined white butterfly the green hue is produced by another method — the overlapping yellow and black scales.

Very rarely in the wild a large white butterfly may be found with a bluish tinge. This is the aberration called ab. *coerulea* which is believed to be due to a recessive gene. Brian Gardiner, the pioneer of synthetic diets for butterflies, soon found that his laboratory stock of the large white had a higher incidence of this aberration than in the wild. Inbreeding increases the chances of its occurring.

Not all plant pigments are coloured. The colourless flavonol pigment called phytoene was detected for the first time in the animal kingdom by this writer in the common blue butterfly. It had come direct from one of its food plants, restharrow (*Ononis repens*). Flavones are directly involved in the 'honey-guides' of plants. They occur where ultra-violet light is absorbed on flower petals. Most of the flavones impart a yellowish colour and must play a role in colouring butterflies in conjunction with the large group of pigments called the carotenoids.

Carotenoids are of widespread occurrence in plant material and there are over 350 different types. In weak concentration they are pale yellow but in increased concentration they produce colours through orange to red. Normally the green chlorophyll of the leaf masks the bright yellow-orange colours of the carotenoids. In vertebrates and invertebrates carotenoids are important as precursors of vitamin A. One molecule of β-carotene is split into two molecules of vitamin A in man. In butterflies this vitamin is implicated in growth, vision, coloration and possibly scent detection.

In both the plant and insect, carotenoids keep most of their physical characteristics. In the plant they pass on light energy to the chlorophylls. In the insect their penchant for coupling onto chemically active compounds is shown in the way they form complexes with proteins (carotenoproteins) — serving to conserve valuable proteins for longer than they would otherwise exist. It is also thought that carotenoids are important in counting time (i.e. for caterpillars likely to form overwintering chrysalises by registering the short days). The yellow, green and orange colours of caterpillars, chrysalises, butterflies and their eggs owe some of their colour to carotenoids. Internally, the fat body (the equivalent of the mammalian liver) and the blood (haemolymph) is coloured yellow due to high concentrations of carotenoids. To get carotenoids into the body they must be selectively stored (sequestered) by the caterpillar at the expense of many other chemicals found in their food plants.

Black and Brown Colours

Black and brown colours are produced by melanin. It is extraordinarily abundant in the animal kingdom and is made by animals from a chemical called tyrosin. It occurs in human skin — allowing us to go brown — in fish skin and in the wings and bodies of butterflies. In weak concentration it gives a brown colour, when concentrated, black. Quite how the metabolic pathway of melanin is organised in the cells is not entirely established.

What we do know is that the black marks of butterflies are mostly melanin; for example, the black spots and tips of the wings of the whites and clouded yellows (*Colias* spp.). Summer butterflies tend to have heavily melanised or black spots compared to those of the spring which are grey. There is an adage which says 'faint, frail and first' meaning that the first generation butterflies tend to be faintly coloured, frail, i.e. non migrants and first, being first generation. The advantage of darker markings in the summer may be a question of providing greater absorption of heat energy — or simply enhancing the bright aposematic colours.

The scales which carry the melanin pigments appear black when seen under the microscope. Occasionally very dark specimens occur. The black fore wing spots of the large white (*Pieris brassicae*) or the small tortoiseshell may be joined giving a darker appearance. In other cases all the wing's surface has a covering of black scales in which case it is called a melanic aberration. The opposite of this is an albino which is either genetically controlled or is a result of a breakdown in the metabolic pathway.

Butterflies which habitually live at high altitudes are often very dark or coloured black. The ringlet *Erebia* butterflies of the mountains of Europe are the best examples. Black absorbs the sun's energy quicker than white so it is useful to the butterfly to be able to warm up quickly in the cooler temperatures up to 2,150 m. There are many examples of ringlets which have black colours such as the Scotch Argus (*Erebia aethiops*) the Arran brown, the manto ringlet (*E. manto*), the sooty ringlet (*E. pluto*), the dryad (*Minois dryas*), or even the black satyr (*Satyrus actaea*) and the great sooty satyr (*Satyrus ferula*). It is not surprising that the mountain ringlets are great sun-bathers. Anyone who has visited a flowery alpine meadow or track will have noticed the erebias with wings wide open whilst they are feeding on the scabious (*Scabiosa* spp.), knapweeds (*Centaurea* spp.) and thistles (*Cirsium* spp.).

Dark-coloured butterflies are also found in the lowlands throughout Europe; butterflies like the ringlet (*Aphantopus hyperantus*) and the meadow brown use their dark colours for secretly hiding in long grass, the black hairstreak (*Strymonidia pruni*) blends in with shadows in the foliage of trees and bushes and the sooty copper (*Heodes tityrus*) is well suited for the waysides where light and dark areas abound. In mountainous areas the Camberwell Beauty (*Nymphalis antiopa*) uses its dark colours to warm up when the sunlight penetrates deep into the damp willow-rich valleys, or when it is sunbathing on a road.

White Colours

Not all butterflies which live at high altitudes are black. The apollos (*Parnassius* spp.) are white and may be found flying alongside the black ringlets. So what is their alternative strategy? They have several features which aid them in keeping warm, their wings have a large number of black spots, their wing bases are black, their bodies are black, they have anti-freeze glycerides in their tissues and they have relatively 'furry' bodies. There is an advantage in seeking out a warm hollow in which to get warmed up quickly. In contrast, during the heat of the day the white areas on the wings of apollos could help reflect heat and keep the body cool. As many apollos are protected species it would be useful to know more about the ecology of these beautiful butterflies.

One of the purest whites seen in butterflies is in the wood white. The small and large white are creamier in comparison and the black-veined white (*Aporia crataegi*) can become rather transparent white. On top of the limestone *causses* of the Central Massif in France I have seen what looks like a 'white-out effect' in some butterflies. In the blazing sun on bleached limestone (which is very tiring on the eyes) butterflies like the hermit (*Chazara briseis*) exist in very light forms indeed. This is paralleled by the grayling (*Hipparchia semele*) in Britain, which in chalk districts exists as a light-coloured form. In both these cases the existence of these colour forms must be attributed to camouflage. However, there is probably another equally important function and that is to prevent desiccation in these very sunny and demanding environments particularly in southern Europe. The light colours help to reflect incident sunlight. The temperature on the baking limestone rocks is high enough to break a normal household thermometer — well in excess of 100°C in direct sunlight.

White colours are produced in a most surprising manner. They are seen principally in the whites and yellows, but also in some of the swallowtails (*Papilio* spp.). The colour comes from their excretory products. The white colour of butterfly wings is made of a waste product called pterin. There are several different types of pterin and they are called pteridines. Instead of being lost from the body they are used for coloration in the wings. Chemically, pterins are similar to the white substance in birds' droppings since they are closely related to uric acid. The yellow urea of human urine is not too distant as this too is a product of protein metabolism.

So the white pterins confer not only a useful coloration but presumably a disagreeable taste to the wings. White is a warning colour and is put to very good use by all the whites, clouded yellows and brimstone (*Gonepteryx rhamni*). Most of these butterflies use their bright colours as a form of advertisement to predators. The mustard oil glycosides of cabbage leaves are also embodied in the wings of white butterflies.

Black and white colours are combined effectively in the marbled white butterflies (*Melanargia* spp.). There are six species in Europe and they vary considerably in their colour. Some appear as if the black spots are on a white background, others white spots on a black background. Despite this, these marbled whites belong to the brown family (Satyridae), whose relatives the ringlets are basically black. To a lesser extent the cabbage whites have a black and white colour scheme but theirs is based on a bias towards the white.

Structural Colours

The blues, coppers and hairstreaks (*Lycaenidae*) show off some of the most spectacular colours seen in butterflies worldwide, and Europe is no exception. These iridescent colours are also called structural colours after the way in which they are formed. There are no plant pigments involved. The iridescence is caused by the light being broken up by the microscopic corrugations on the surface of the wing scales. It is the males which have the largest amount of iridescent colour on the wings. It is needed for sexual recognition. In many species the female has completely different colours and patterns. Indeed, many females of the blues are actually brown. They have to keep out of the way of predators so that they can safely lay their eggs and it is an advantage not to be seen with very obvious colours. In species like the scarce copper (*Heodes virgaureae*) and the large blue (*Maculinea arion*) the female is quite unlike the male and covered in spots rather than a complete sheen of colour.

Figure 5.1   Male Adonis blues 'mud-puddling'

Brightly-coloured males are also seen in the purple emperor (*Apatura iris*), the females being a discreet brown colour. The structural purple colour varies according to the incidence of the light and it is thought that this is due to melanin pigments in the scales. There is a subtle purple bloom over the wings of the southern white admiral (*Ladoga reducta*) which appears at certain angles probably due to the same mechanism.

Spots and Eyespots

Butterflies have a marvellous array of spots on their wings, ranging from individual spots, rows of spots and wings covered with numerous dark blotches. The latter are not regarded as spots, but those towards the tip of the fore wing are known as eyespots. At the tip of the fore wing the spot is also called a discal spot. Eyespots are the false eyes displayed on butterfly wings. In most butterflies they mimic vertebrate eyes and may or may not be pupilled. They vary from large 1 cm diameter eyespots to small spots on the wing. And they can be either on the upper or lower surface of the fore or hind wing. The browns are specialists at eyespots on both sides of the fore wing, the swallowtails and hairstreaks have developed special spots at the base of their 'tails' and the nymphalids have one species, the peacock (*Inachis io*), which has taken its eyespots to a very high degree of evolution. The functional importance of butterfly eyespots is as deflection characteristics to persuade a bird to peck at a dispensible part. That this clearly works is seen in nature as butterflies with beak and claw marks near the tip of the fore wings are frequently seen.

In the grayling and the great banded grayling (*Brintesia circe*) the discal eyespot is sometimes withdrawn out of view behind the hind wing especially for concealment immediately on landing. It is crucial for many butterflies to blend in with the terrain or woodland trees on which they settle as soon as they alight. When the great banded grayling settles on a tree and withdraws its fore wings between its hind wings it is very difficult to see.

The four large eyespots of the peacock are designed to startle a predator. They are used quickly to deter a predator whilst the insect does not give any ground. They have been evolved by an invertebrate to scare off a very much more potent vertebrate; no mean feat for a humble butterfly. The apollo butterfly (*Parnassius apollo*) also has two distinctive eyespots on the hind wing and these are used to frighten predators. Both the apollo and the peacock are specialists at audio-visual deterrent systems. When a predator approaches, the butterfly stays still, opens its wings and makes a sound. Sound in the peacock is made by rubbing its wings together; that in the apollo is from two sources, first, from rubbing the undersides of its hind wings against its resting place and second, a hissing snake-like sound by scraping the back of its legs against the base of the wing. Furthermore the apollo 'blinks' with its large eyespots by repeatedly raising and lowering its fore wings.

Other butterflies employ a nauseous secretion derived from the food plant in combination with their warning coloration. But in the peacock and other related nymphalids there is no reason to suppose that they employ poisonous compounds to back up their bright colours and eyespots. The bright colours found in a typical peacock's eyespots are due to structural colours. Nettles are not noted for toxic chemicals which could be used by butterflies for defence.

Figure 5.2   A variety of eyespots is seen in butterflies from three families, the browns, the swallowtails and the nymphalids

Fritillaries are so called, like the plants of the same name, after their spottedness, which covers all surfaces of their wings. Most of the fritillaries are butterflies which fly around in light woodland, clearings, woodland margins and along tracks. Here the sunlight percolates down through the undergrowth and spots onto leaves creating areas of light and dark. It is in this speckled environment that the woodland fritillaries (and other woodland species too) have evolved their spottedness. The usefulness of the spottedness of fritillaries' wings is, therefore, immediately apparent. The varying patches of light and dark over the wings comes in very useful since they are (presumably) less easily seen. A butterfly like the marbled fritillary (*Brenthis daphne*) which flies lazily around bramble patches, or the spotted fritillary (*Melitaea didyma*) and the Queen of Spain fritillary (*Issoria lathonia*) which fly repeatedly up and down partially-shaded waysides are well suited to this particular environment.

The use of a mass of spots or blotches is seen in several butterflies, particularly the blues, marbled whites and the speckled wood (*Pararge aegeria*). There is very little functional difference between a wing full of spots and one full of light and dark-coloured blotches or patches. Only the spots of the speckled wood are fairly constant. For butterflies living in open grassland habitats and within woods the patterns are likely to be the same, for instance the amount of shade within tall grasses is fairly similar to habitats along forest edges or in woodland clearings.

The spottedness of the meadow brown was extensively studied by W.H. Dowdeswell and much of this work, with Professor E.B. Ford, is explained in his admirable *The Life of the Meadow Brown* (1981). This butterfly is one of the commonest butterflies throughout western Europe and both sexes have eyespots, though they are, exceptionally, more pronounced in the female. Dowdeswell investigated the variability of spotting throughout Europe; was there any variation throughout its range? Well the answer was yes. The spottedness of this butterfly is remarkably stable throughout much of its range, but at the periphery it varies from the norm; in Dowdeswell's words 'the genes controlling spotting and its characteristic patterns appear to be trans-specific, trans-generic, trans-familial, and therefore of great antiquity'. With Professor Kennedy McWhirter, Dowdeswell looked at all specimens from Europe in the collection of the British Museum (Natural History) covering 1890–1936. The spotting varied in isolated places in Ireland, on islands like the Scillies and the Canaries as well as on the three peninsulas of Iberia, Italy and Greece.

Back to Front Mimicry

A number of butterflies from the swallowtail and Lycaenidae family have separately evolved the effective device of mimicking their own head and antennae. It is a specialised state of eyespot evolution used in combination with butterfly 'tails'. A side look at the swallowtail, the scarce swallowtail (*Iphiclides podalirius*) the long-tailed blue (*Lampides boeticus*) or the brown, purple or ilex hairstreak (*Thecla betulae, Quercusia quercus, Nordmannia ilicis*) will show this interesting phenomenon well. Those of the long-tailed blue are particularly distinct, with the 'tails' twisted and the 'eyes' very clear. In the Lycaenidae the tails are never long and are not always present. The small copper (*Lycaena phlaeas*) may or may not have the 'tails' slightly developed.

By making a dummy set of head and antennae on their posterior end,

Figure 5.3   The scarce swallowtail is a specialist at back-to-front mimicry, even confusing humans

these butterflies have effectively increased their survival rate. When a bird is coming into the attack on one of these butterflies it is confronted with two possible alternatives for the front end, i.e., from its point of view, where the 'meat' is. So there is a very good chance that the bird may well choose the wrong end and only get a mouthful of unnutritious wing. The important thing is that the butterfly has survived the attack. It is of secondary importance that it may be minus its alluring decorations. In their short lives an extra day is very significant. As with woodland and hedgerow butterflies, which become torn on brambles, they can still fly around even with two thirds of their wings gone. In the scarce swallowtail the dummy head and antennae appear to be more conspicuous than the real head and antennae. This presumably increases the chances that an attack will be sustained at the rear of the body than at the front. The chances of the butterfly surviving an attack would seem to be in excess of 50 per cent.

There are other forms of mimicry in European Lepidoptera, namely Batesian and Müllerian, both named after the entomologists who proposed them. Batesian mimicry relies upon a poisonous model and a palatable mimic which has evolved a similar aposematic colour to the model. Predators soon learn to associate a bad experience with a particular colour scheme when they tackle the model and thereafter they overlook the mimic. There are no recorded cases of Batesian mimicry in Europe amongst butterflies. In contrast, there are good examples of Müllerian mimicry in European butterflies. Müllerian mimicry exists over a very large area and involves several species. Here several species have simultaneously evolved a similar colour scheme. The best example is seen in the whites. They nearly all have a white or yellowish colour with black or grey marks or spots. The whites looks very much the same from a distance anywhere between western Europe and China so it is a very widespread phenomenon. Their defence is dependent upon the poisons stored in their bodies and wings.

The cabbage whites also have pterin substances in their wings as well as their mustard oil glycosides derived from the caterillar food plants. The complex of butterflies exhibiting Müllerian mimicry is upheld by the predators since the butterflies have these substances as their major toxic deterrent. Many other whites, like the orange tip or green-veined white, do not feed on toxic plants, so they are presumably deriving protection by looking like the other commoner species.

Zig-zags, Lines and Bands

The use of these patterns is seen in several butterfly families. It is particularly well represented in the swallowtails, with alternating bands of black and white or black and yellow. In the festoons (*Zerynthia* spp.) the margins of the wings are distinctly scalloped. Where bands occur they are generally next to dark colours which make the juxtaposition of colours contrasting. In the Eastern European gliders (*Neptis* spp.) and the admirals (white, red and poplar, *Vanessa* and *Ladoga* spp.) there are bands of white on the fore wings. All these devices must be a form of advertisement. The butterflies 'want' to be seen by predators and rely on their learned behaviour. Some may be loaded with plant poisons, others may not. There is therefore plenty of room for mimicry. In butterfly-rich habitats, the great array of rich colours are very important for intra-specific recognition, i.e. so that members of different species can recognise each other.

The festoons are non-migratory butterflies which are often restricted to isolated meadows and spend much of their time resting on vegetation. To us they can be very difficult to find when at rest. Their pattern is effective at breaking up their outline and making them less obvious. But when flying or basking with wings open they show off their bright colours (red, white and black marks). As they all feed as caterpillars on birthworts (*Aristolochia* spp.) it is highly likely that these butterflies have aristolochic acids as part of their chemical defence, but this has not been ascertained.

The boldest bands are seen in the nymphalids. The creamy band on the margins of the wings of the Camberwell Beauty are enormously effective when in flight. They contrast strongly with the dark areas of the wings and must be for recognition and perhaps advertisement. When a butterfly like this passes into shade, only the creamy bands are conspicuous. This is seen more effectively in the rainforests when butterflies of a similar colouring fly into pitch-black shade. One wonders whether the magnificent Camberwell Beauty butterflies have salicilic acid in their bodies derived from the willows (*Salix* spp.) on which the caterpillars feed. By comparison the orange bands on the wing margins of the two-tailed pasha (*Charaxes jasius*) are not particularly distinctive, at least to us. Speed and great evasive action when under attack may be more important to these butterflies.

6 Habitats

Come where the Hair-streak flutters by
Like a living leaf; where the butterfly
Whose snowy wings are dash'd with green,
And with rich orange tipp'd, is seen,
Where the Chequer'd Skipper, as you tread,
Springs lightly from its grassy
bed, . . .

T.F. (1861) *An Invitation to the Woods*
In the *Entomologist's Weekly Intelligencer*

INTRODUCTION

In this chapter there is a heavy emphasis on botany since plants are used to describe habitats and butterflies are often restricted to particular habitats because of certain food plants. What we learnt in Chapter 4 on butterfly food plants is important too since plants will only grow in certain types of soil.

Very few detailed studies of butterfly habitats have been done. Gomez-Bustillo and Rubio's mid-1970s work on the butterflies and moths of the Iberian Peninsula is useful since it illustrates several habitat types and associated species though it is more important for moths than butterflies. Henriksen and Kreutzer's *The Butterflies of Scandinavia in Nature* (1982) is a gold mine of information, not only for its descriptions of butterfly habitats, but also for the photographs of the habitat of each of the butterflies described. John Heath (*et al*) in his *Atlas of Butterflies in Britain and Ireland* (1984) gives us the most up-to-date information on the ecology of British butterflies. Heath's book is published by the Institute of Terrestrial Ecology (I.T.E.) as is *Butterfly Research in I.T.E.* (1981) by Marney Hall which provides an interesting study of the ecology of seven species of butterfly. Balletto and his colleagues diligently checked out 750 butterfly habitats in Italy including the major islands of Elba, Sardinia and Sicily and recorded the presence of 234 species. The richest butterfly habitat was the lower montane ecological zone with 152 species and the poorest was alpine grassland with 29 species.

Despite this work already done on butterfly habitats it is painfully obvious that precious little is actually known about most of the habitat requirements of European butterflies. This chapter draws attention to the way soil, aspect and temperature affect habitats, and how butterflies adapt to the ever changing nature of habitats.

A number of people are associated with particular butterflies since they have made detailed ecological studies of various species. However, the number of species studied is all too few; Eric Duffey with the swallowtail (*Papilio machaon*) and large copper (*Lycaena dispar*), Stephen Courtney with the orange tip (*Anthocharis cardamines*), N.B. Davies with the speckled wood (*Pararge aegeria*), Dietrich Magnus with the silver-washed fritillary (*Argynnis paphia*), Keith Porter with the marsh fritillary (*Euphydryas aurinia*) and Jeremy Thomas with the large blue (*Maculinea arion*).

Plants are not only used to describe habitats but are used as indicators to show how old and undisturbed a habitat might be. The older or more original/relic a habitat is, the more wild plant species are present. This, of course, provides plenty of food plant for caterpillars and we might expect several more butterfly species in an ancient habitat than a new one. However, there are plenty of examples of new man-made habitats being colonised by butterflies where they then become abundant.

SOILS

Butterflies have great powers of adaptation and have exploited many different types of habitat from alpine meadow to lowland bog. In any investigation of butterfly habitats we continually come back to considering what type of soil is present in a locality. The standard textbooks of ecological botany tell us which plants grow on what soils, so, armed with information on butterfly food plants we soon learn where to expect one sort of butterfly or another. It is a very good idea to study a geological map of your country or county. Many of the habitats that we associate with butterflies — coppices, hedgerows, forestry rides and urban areas — are aritificial in origin or man-made. This suggests immediately that butterflies are expert colonisers of new types of habitat. There are even rare species of butterfly which frequent grassy roadside refuges.

But where did butterflies live before there was this wide array of inviting habitats? What were the ancient, relic or original habitats that butterflies used to live in even before man was around 2 million years ago? Again the answer lies in the soil type. We know that much of the countryside was covered with forest 5,000 years ago. We have evidence from pollen analysis of peat about the change in vegetation over the last few thousand years. Different species of tree have had their eras of dominance over the years, their success or not governed by the vagaries of the climate. Populations of butterflies have waxed and waned with the Ice Ages up to 10,000 years ago.

Most of the land mass would have been covered with forest, especially over clay or chalky soils. Limestones would have had low, fairly sparse woodland, similar one imagines to the Burren in western Ireland or some of the limestone *causse* areas of the Massif Central in France. Both these limestone areas are fairly open habitats, more so the Continental limestone areas. Many butterfly species would have lived along the forest margins and clearings. There are so many factors about the forest or

1. A male silver-spotted skipper
   (Ochlodes venata)

2. Plain tiger *(Danaus chrysippus)*

3. The apollo *(Parnassius apollo)*

4. The southern festoon *(Zerynthia polyxena)*

5. The Moroccan orange tip
(Anthocharis belia)

6. The wood white *(Leptidea sinapis)*

7. Black-veined whites *(Aporia crataegi)*

8. The brimstone *(Gonepteryx rhamni)*

9. A female small white *(Pieris rapae)*

10. The peacock *(Inachis io)*

11. The painted lady *(Cynthia cardui)* 12. The southern white admiral
(Ladoga reducta)

13. The silver-washed fritillary *(Argynnis paphia)*

14. The heath fritillary *(Mellicta athalia)*

15. The male common blue *(Polyommatus icarus)*

16. The long-tailed blue
    (Lampides boeticus)

17. The black satyr *(Satyrus actaea)*

18. The Arran brown *(Erebia ligea)*

19. The scarce copper *(Heodes virgaureae)*

20. The green hairstreak *(Callophrys rubi)*

woodland edge which makes it attractive as a place for evolution: shelter, sunlight and a wider range of wild plant species than found inside the wood. Butterflies would have colonised the woods; a very easy exercise in places like the amazing dwarf native hazel woods of western Ireland where there is little boundary between edge and wood. Soon woodland species would have evolved.

As in human evolution the woodland margin was vital in separating distinct populations of animals. Some individuals would have stayed in the wood, others remained on the margin. We can see today butterflies which fit these two habitats, speckled woods in the woods and hedge browns (*Pyronia* spp.) along the margin or rides, which are, after all, only extensions of the margin.

Ever since man has been on earth the amount of woodland and forest has been declining. More open natural or semi-natural grasslands have been created. Most butterfly species live on grassland, heaths, moors and mountain meadows. Many may prosper in the man-made urban garden habitat. Very few actually live in the woods. Plenty are found along margins, rides, glades and hedgerows.

All this suggests that butterflies evolved in the grassland or margin and then speciated into the woods. It is quite feasible — in the absence of any real fossil evidence — that butterflies evolved in a mixed habitat of woods and grassy clearings, perhaps fashioned by fire or other natural cause.

In beechwoods another factor comes into play which provides further clearings for butterflies. The sycamore (*Acer pseudoplatanus*) creates a disruptive influence on the climax communities of beech. Sycamore is native to central and southern Europe yet it was introduced into Britain in the fifteenth or sixteenth century and is now naturalised. Where a beech tree fell down and created a clearing, young beech (*Fagus sylvatica*) and ash (*Fraxinus excelsior*) seedlings would compete for the light and eventually beech would succeed and close the clearing gap. Now that sycamore is present it competes more successfully with ash and beech and ousts the other two. Progressively the climax state of the beech wood is destroyed, further beech trees become isolated and more vulnerable to the effect of wind. More trees fall over and more clearings are formed.

CLIMATE, WEATHER AND ASPECT

In western Europe there are four different types of climate that influence butterflies: Atlantic, Mediterranean, Continental and Arctic. Each area has typical butterfly species, although there are species which are found in several of these climatic regions. Some butterflies are clearly capable of living in several different climates, whilst others are strictly governed by their regional climatic conditions.

Substantial changes in climate, such as occurred during the Ice Ages, had profound effects on butterflies. Many species died out. As the ice advanced south, ice caps formed over the present day Alps, Pyrénées and Massif Central and the tundra and cold-temperate zone advanced with it. This would kill off (or drive further south) the warm-temperate species and sub-Arctic species would take their place. When the ice retreated, this was reversed. These ice movements had a profound effect on the distribution of some butterflies, like the boreo-alpine species, that we see today. Some butterfly species are now only found in the far north of Europe and high on the mountains of the south, but not in the intervening lowlands. This is explained by supposing that (being conditioned to cold habitat) they were spread in the lowlands, south of the ice-sheet, during glacial phases of the Ice Age, but in interglacial periods, such as the present day, they retreated, on the one hand, northwards and, on the other hand up the mountains, disappearing in the intervening temperature lowlands. The alpine grizzled skipper (*Pyrgus andromedae*) and the dewy ringlet (*Erebia pandrose*) are good examples, both occurring in the Alps, Pyrénées and at sea level in Scandinavia. The dewy ringlet occurs along much of Norway's mountain range, in the lowland areas north of the Gulf of Bothnia, and up to the Arctic Sea.

There is a similar analogous situation used to describe the demise of wild plants or butterflies in cornfields 'that they have been driven to the edges of the fields' through the widespread use of herbicides. They have simply been killed off in the centre of the field and only the populations of plants or butterflies which always lived at the edge of the field survive to perpetuate the species (if they too hadn't been herbicided). Intensive agriculture concentrates species into isolated woods and ragged escarpments — refuges for wildlife in a sea of sterile agricultural land. It is the fortunate populations of plants and animals that survive in these 'island populations' that save the day for that particular species.

Some botanists and entomologists believe that, during the Ice Ages the tops of some of the highest mountains within ice-bound northern Europe would have protruded out of the ice sheet and been bathed in glorious sunshine. This theory of protruding 'nunataks' is proposed to account for the present-day distribution of alpine plant species in Scotland and north Wales. It is possible that some alpine butterflies also sought refuge here, with their food plants, and remained with viable populations until the ice cap melted. This theory is used to account for the presence of some butterflies in Scotland and their absence further south in England. There is also evidence from the distribution of lichens and flowering plants, some of which are only found in the highest points in the Massif Central, the Alps or in the Scottish Highlands.

The climate is always changing by such small incremental units each year that it is often not possible for us to detect it. Sometimes there is a gradual deterioration or amelioration in the climate. Many forms of wildlife are affected. When the climate becomes gradually colder, birds, marine mammals and insects move southwards. The reverse is true when the climate becomes a little better. For many insect species as well as plants, the British Isles represent a fragile foothold in their northern range. Some species which occur in southern England may well die off and be found only along the northern parts of France when the climate becomes slightly worse. The Lulworth skipper (*Thymelicus acteon*) and Glanville fritillary (*Melitaea cinxia*) are good examples which show a fragile hold in Britain.

Aspect of the land can have a profound effect on the flight times of butterflies. An 'early' south-facing site can be as much as three to four weeks ahead of a 'late' north-facing site because it receives much more of the incident sunlight. The sun plays such an important role in the life of butterflies (see also Chapters 7 and 8). The insects on an 'early' site are active earlier and later in the day than on a 'late' site. The benefit of extra energy in plant growth is passed on to caterpillar development.

Around the coast 'miniaturisation' of plants is frequently found. Plants subjected to the damaging effects of prevailing winds and salt spray have evolved diminutive forms which cope with these conditions. Some butterflies have done exactly the same. There are dwarf forms of the silver-studded blue (*Plebejus argus*) — some 4 mm less wingspan than normal — and the grayling (*Hipparchia semele*) which lives in north Wales. The dwarf forms of the silver-studded blue (form *caernensis*) live on the coastal limestone of Gwynedd and those of the grayling (form *thyone*), on Great Orme's Head (Gwynedd). Development time of the caterpillars takes a little longer under these conditions, and adults emerge a few weeks later than the typical inland forms in order to complete their life cycle in time. The small copper (*Lycaena phlaeas*) is also known in a small form (*minimus*) from unimproved pasture. One nymphalid, the dark green fritillary, (*Argynnis aglaja*) can cope with the windy conditions on coastal cliffs where there is plenty of short grass and scrub and its violet (*Viola*) food plants.

HABITAT CHANGE

No habitat stands still and remains just how you saw it on one particular day. You may have a recollection of a choice habitat brim full of butterflies on a fine sunny day. Is it the same now? Habitats are *always* changing. There is a gradual plant succession which occurs in all habitats until a 'climax community' is established. A grassland will develop scrub and eventually trees, a wet meadow will become invaded with alder (*Alnus* sp.) and willow (*Salix* sp.), an embryo dune will change into a mature dune system with pine (*Pinus* spp.) trees.

So what are these ancient, relic and natural habitats that people like to associate with rich wildlife? In forests they are areas which support a diverse collection of plants, in the herb, field and shrub layers. Certain wild plants, mosses, lichens and ferns are called 'indicator species'. Many plants come in association with each other — a typical example is red

Figure 6.1   The swallowtail is particularly sensitive to a drying-out of its wetland habitat, particularly in Britain

campion (*Silene dioica*), greater stitchwort (*Stellaria neglecta*) and bluebell (*Endymion non-scriptus*). It takes an experienced eye to note all the particular species but the first step is to be able to identify most of the flowering and non-flowering plants. You can get a very good idea about a possible ancient woodland by consulting old maps. If woods had not been grubbed out before about 1600 and they are still there today, the wood is very likely to be ancient. Ancient habitats are renowned for their plant diversity; beetles and butterflies form part of that richness.

Each habitat can be defined exactly by its particular flora so it is easy to formulate a picture of a habitat in your mind. Once seen on the ground it is difficult to erase the uniqueness of a thick oak woodland or the bare openness of a beechwood. Climax communities, as the name suggests, indicate that a stable condition has been attained; in fact it may stay relatively unchanged for thousands of years. But there is an exception. With beechwoods a breakdown of this stable condition eventually occurs, usually through intense fungal activity, and this results in an 'over-mature' state; trees suffer from beech-snap, and make more clearings for butterflies to colonise. It is interesting that some conservation-minded foresters now actually put clearings into thick and uninteresting stands of conifers in order to keep the wildlife value of an area rich.

Populations of butterflies which live in woodland clearings are only there temporarily. In a natural wood a clearing would soon be absorbed into the fabric of the whole woodland, but fortunately in man-managed habitats such as coppice woods, butterflies can, with luck, survive in these refuges. Ironically, conservation of nature reserves rich in butterflies, often means stopping the natural processes which occur in plant succession. The philosophy towards nature conservation in some countries, such as Britain, is very much geared towards keeping at all costs flower-rich or butterfly-rich meadows — and fighting plant succession.

There are other changes which affect habitats and man is often the influencing factor. Grazing stops any tendency for a grassland type of habitat to change. Young scrub bushes are eaten off and a fine sward of grasses takes over from coarse grasses. This may have a profound effect on the types of butterfly present. Whether it is bullocks, sheep or rabbits grazing the effect is the same, although they vary in their selectivity of feeding. There is much to be said for grazing as an important conservation tool which removes scrub and increases the fertility of the soil. Grazing and conservation of butterflies definitely go hand in hand.

When something upsets the *status quo* of habitats, whether it is man-induced or natural, problems for butterflies can result. Rabbits and myxomatosis were both introduced by man. Butterflies thrived in the well-nibbled pastures, but when rabbits disappeared due to myxomatosis, plant succession took over. Grasslands disappeared under scrub and light woodland developed. The large blue became extinct in 1979 in Britain, and other species such as the small heath (*Coenonympha pamphilus*) and ringlets (*Aphantopus hyperantus*) died out in some localities indirectly due to myxomatosis.

OTHER ECOLOGICAL FACTORS

There are other ecological factors to take into consideration when studying butterfly habitats. First, that some butterflies only seem to require just a small 'oasis' of suitable habitat to sustain a viable population (see Chapter 8). This is often much smaller than lepidopterists think. Obviously, if the habitat meets the correct 'habitat criteria' of the butterfly the chances of the butterfly raising a viable population are higher. Choice habitats may be few and far between so that the sort of philosophy of 'putting all your eggs in the same basket' obviously works. The phenomenon also occurs elsewhere in nature, particularly in birds, reptiles and amphibians.

Some butterflies are not restricted to one habitat alone. The brimstone (*Gonepteryx rhamni*) changes its preference with age; first seeking out a habitat in the open for nectar and then later searching woodlands and downland for its food plant — the buckthorns (*Rhamnus* spp.). Other butterflies, like the small tortoiseshell (*Aglais urticae*), the red admiral (*Vanessa atalanta*), the clouded yellow (*Colias croceus*) and the painted lady (*Cynthia cardui*) are seen in many different habitats.

Whether habitats are large or small they are vital to the life of butterflies. If you cannot define the habitat requirements of a butterfly you cannot hope to conserve them. Very few of the butterflies in western Europe have had their habitats analysed from the butterfly's point of view.

GRASSLANDS

Grassland is the habitat with which most butterfly species are associated. Grassland includes not only grassy clearings in woods, but open moor-like habitats with extensive grassland cover as well as man-made grassy motorway embankments, parks and wilder gardens. The butterflies most likely to be found here are the skippers and browns which utilise the grasses as food plants. The Lycaenidae are well represented too since their caterpillars exploit the vetches and docks growing alongside the grasses. It has already been stressed that several of these grass-dependent butterflies lay their eggs while flying, since grass is readily available and not too difficult to find and the caterpillars may use several grass species as food plants.

There are several different types of grassland habitats. The high altitude windswept plateaux in Europe contrast strongly with the rolling countryside of southern England. Skippers seem to be equally at home in very wild and exposed places as in sheltered woodland glades. The browns seem not to be so tolerant; they prefer the more sheltered areas.

Sheltered grassland habitats such as those that occur in hollows on chalk soils, for instance on the Downs or Chilterns in England or in Picardy in northern France, offer ideal habitats for butterflies. Out of the wind the sun beats down into these natural hollows creating greater activity in the butterflies and presumably ample supplies of nectar in the wild flowers. Many butterfly species can be seen in such ideal situations — blues, coppers, marbled whites and browns.

Some butterflies like the grass short, others like it long, so the presence or absence of grazers is important. The silver-spotted skipper (*Hesperia comma*) likes the grass sward extremely short. This may be produced by grazing rabbits or, as a widespread practice in upland Europe, grazing of large flocks of sheep or goats. The ancient Continental practice of taking sheep up to higher pastures in the summer (*transhumance*) to benefit from the new growth of grass results in many areas being kept down to a fine turf. Combined with the hot Mediterranean climate grasses parch out but still support populations of silver-spotted skipper. The butterfly also thrives in rural lowland areas where goats are efficient grazers. In contrast the large skipper (*Ochlodes venata*) prefers habitats where the grass is much longer. Perhaps a woodland glade, ride or hedgerow path where the grass is growing around ditches or in the rougher areas.

Both the small skipper (*Thymelicus sylvestris*) and the Essex skipper (*Thymelicus lineola*) are expert colonisers of man-made habitats, such as roads, dual-carriageways and motorway embankments. Man has inadvertently created these grasslands which can be looked upon as linear nature reserves. The grass-feeding caterpillars of these skipper butterflies have found a bonanza. The grassy wastes are rarely managed — except to keep sight-lines open — and are infrequently cut or sprayed with herbicides. I well remember finding thousands of Essex skippers living on the motorway embankments of the M20 in Kent in 1978 when I carried out a biological survey with Eric Philp. To everyone's surprise these and 14 other butterfly species were thriving well on what appeared to be an unremarkable motorway embankment. Incidentally, Essex skippers are certainly not restricted to Essex in their distribution. They are exceedingly overlooked and consequently under-recorded since they are mistaken for small skippers.

One of the other butterflies that had found its way onto the motorway verge was the ringlet. It's a reclusive sort of butterfly and apparently not an active flier. But it had obviously made the exploratory flights necessary to get itself onto a motorway verge in the first place across inhospitable agricultural land. The ringlets prefer the damper grasslands, hollows and wet meadows enclosed by tall trees. Another butterfly of wetter areas is the dingy skipper (*Erynnis tages*) but it flies also in dunes and heaths and limestone areas.

Sand dune areas are grassy habitats of little general use to butterflies. Most of the grasses are coarse species which withstand salt and wind, for example, marram grass (*Ammophilia* spp.), and are not generally exploited as caterpillar food plants. The other occasional grasses which occur occasionally like fescues (*Festuca* sp.) and couch grass (*Agropyron* sp.) in the more mature dune system support some browns and skippers and the wild crucifers and sea lavenders (*Limonium* spp.) provide nectar sources for migrants. In Britain there are no species of butterflies confined to dunes, though the caterpillars of the grayling have been found on marram grass in Lancashire. In Holland, however, the tree grayling (*Neohipparchia statilinus*) is now restricted to six localities in inland sand dunes or driftsands. It requires a habitat rich in lichens, heather and bare sand.

HEATHLAND

Heathlands are one of the most threatened habitats in western Europe. So many have been lost completely to urbanisation, or ploughing up in the process of 'improving' the land. Those that remain, particularly those under military control, are now demonstrating that there are more butterfly species present there than in other similar-sized areas of the so-called countryside (see Chapter 10). The amount of heathland remaining in southern England is plummeting to a mere fraction of what was there in the middle of the last century. Many of the former rich collecting grounds of the Victorians, such as the New Forest and the Dorset heathlands in general, have gone forever.

Heathlands contain heather (*Calluna vulgaris*) and heaths (*Erica* spp.) of which there are several species. Interspersed there may be pine (*Pinus* spp.), gorse (*Ulex europaeus*) and broom (*Sarothamnus scoparius*), a typical vegetation of an acid soil. Where the ground is light and sandy the opportunist silver birch (*Betula pendula*) grows. Numerous saplings of these quick-growing species provide scrub, shelter and a habitat for some butterflies.

Grassland dominates much of heathland and not surprisingly the skippers and brown butterflies thrive. The grayling is a fast-flying butterfly which does not mind the gusty conditions sometimes found on heathlands. Small heaths and small skippers may also be present. In wetter areas near streams the docks and trefoils support small coppers and dingy skippers (*Erynnis tages*).

Grasslands at altitudes above 1,000 m are frequently colonised by the ringlet butterflies of the *Erebia* genus of which there are over 40 species in Europe. These are dark brown butterflies with reddish markings and eyespots on the wings. Being dark they absorb the sunlight energy, essential at this altitude where the weather is not always warm.

WOODLANDS

Oakwoods

Oakwoods are very rich open habitats compared to beechwoods since the tree canopies do not completely interlock and shut out the light. This means that sunlight pours down through the gaps in the canopy and encourages plants to grow from the woodland floor. Thickets of vegetation occur and the general effect, especially in a typical British oakwood (of common, pedunculate or English oak, *Quercus robur*), is that you cannot see through it very far. The same situation is also found throughout northern Europe. Oakwoods usually develop on clay, rarely on chalk or limestone. The only time you will find oakwoods in chalky areas is where the soil has an overlay of clay with flints.

In southern Europe other oaks are involved and the situation is slightly different. The typical green of the Mediterranean hills and mountains is due to the holly and pubescent oaks (*Quercus ilex* and *Quercus pubescens*). The mature trees in these natural woods tend to be stunted in growth due to the oppressive heat and summer drought conditions and they provide a fairly open and sunny type of habitat for butterflies. Plenty of tall grasses growing round these trees attract several butterfly species. The plantations of cork oak (*Quercus suber*) in Spain also provide ample space for butterflies between the large trees.

Some of the largest and most impressive butterflies live in oakwoods. These include the emperor butterflies (*Apatura* spp.), the largest of the fritillaries (*Argynnis* spp.) and the white admiral (*Lagoda camilla*). They all like sunspots in the wood; places where the sunlight plays on brambles, leaves and where it is warm and sheltered.

Much has been written about the habitat requirements of the purple emperor; especially by Ian Heslop and his colleagues in the 1960s. Large mature oak trees are favoured by the purple emperor for feeding and territorial behaviour. Trees about 9 to 12 m high seem to catch their attention. The butterflies use so-called 'dropping-off points' or perches from which they sally forth through the branches to sallow (*Salix spp.*) which generally has to be in the shade if it is likely to be used for egg-laying. Heslop argued that the oakwood has to be of the dense variety, specifically not the open type. He proposed that 122 to 162 ha was sufficient to maintain a viable population of about 1,000 individuals.

The male purple emperor imbibes its vital nutrients from organic matter on the woodland floor: as Heslop says it is 'easily captured while enjoying the luxurious juice of a dead cat, stoat or rabbit, or of a seething mass of pig's dung', but it will also drink at fox droppings or the juice from gamekeepers' larders. Its penchant for rotting flesh was its downfall in Victorian times when rotten meat was hung up to entice it down from its perch points high in the canopy. Over 100 were taken in an Essex wood in a fortnight — nets 9 to 12 m long were used to collect the butterflies from the heights — 'it sits on some projecting spray in right royal state, and where is the puny entomologist with rod and net shall reach it down from thence?'

The white admiral also selects certain trees in oakwoods; the same trees selected by different individuals every year. They are July fliers and several may be found in a sheltered corner where the sunlight plays down on to generous clumps of bramble (*Rubus* spp.). Perhaps eight or nine butterflies cavort around the playground area all the time that the sun shines. Some sit high in the oak canopy sipping honeydew from the aphid-strewn leaves (*A. iris* does this too), others imbibe nectar from the bramble flowers whilst others launch themselves into circuits between the canopy and the woodland floor disturbing others which join in the fray. Some females depart to go egg-laying in the wood. In some areas they choose the

Figure 6.2   Honeysuckle is the only food plant for the caterpillars of the white admiral

large knots of honeysuckle (*Lonicera* spp.) which scramble up certain trees; in contrast they choose the delicate strands of honeysuckle which creep across the woodland floor in other woods.

In the Mediterranean the great-banded grayling (*Brintesia circe*) is as much at home in a wood as any butterfly; it is large, with a wingspan of 8 cm. When disturbed it flies off rapidly to alight on a tree trunk further on. It pulls its fore wings between its hind wings, like so many other Satyridae, and becomes effectively camouflaged. However, it is easily disturbed and will go on flying and hiding indefinitely. It has all the characteristics of a butterfly much adapted to life within a wood. The woodland grayling (*Hipparchia fagi*) also lives in woods and has much the same behaviour as *H. circe*.

One of the most researched woodland butterflies in Britain is the speckled wood (*Pararge aegeria tircis*) which exists in an orange coloured form called *P.a. aegeria* in southern Europe. It chooses sunlit corners in oakwoods where it fiercely (as much as butterflies can) protects its territory. It is not entirely restricted to woods since it is also found amongst the willow-lined river valleys in Continental Europe.

No oakwood would be complete without its range of fritillaries. Sadly the woodland glades of south-east England have much fewer of the large fritillaries, particularly the high brown (*Argynnis adippe*) which once were a traditional part of the countryside that somebody like Gilbert White must have taken for granted. Being principally an ornithologist he did not get much in the way of entomological information down on paper and did not mention these woodland butterflies. Many of the mountainous and rural areas of central Europe have a complement of wildlife today which mirrors that of the British countryside over 100 years ago. What our forebears saw can be seen today in several remote areas of Europe. The violets that support so many of the fritillaries live on the mossy banks and tracks through the woods, as well as elsewhere along hedgerows and banks. The fritillaries may also be found in open scrubby areas adjacent to woods where there is perhaps equal proportions of grass and scrub. The dark green fritillary is known to perch in trees when it rains.

One of the few butterflies whose food plant is oak is the purple hairstreak (*Quercusia quercus*). It is widespread throughout Europe and sometimes several can be found basking around one small area. In England it often frequents the tops of oak trees and is consequently out of the reach of collectors (much to its benefit — an ideal conservation strategy). In southern Europe relatively small oak bushes, 2 m high, can be found with five or six purple hairstreaks cavorting about. Its caterpillars are ideally adapted for life on the oak since they resemble buds. The Spanish purple hairstreak (*Laeosopis roboris*) is only linked to the purple hairstreak by its English name. It is part of a separate genus but its caterpillars do not feed on oak as its specific name, *roboris* might otherwise have suggested. Instead they feed on ash which is not related to oak.

The ilex hairstreaks (*Nordmannia ilicis* and *esculi*) are good examples of insects co-evolved with their food plants, the holly oakwoods of the Mediterranean. They spend the night resting at the top of scrub bushes like juniper (*Juniperus* spp.) together with species like the blue-spot hairstreak (*Strymonidia spini*) — an impressive species whose food plant is buckthorn (*Rhamnus* spp.).

In a typical English oakwood there are sometimes as many as 15 other species of tree growing side by side with the dominant oak. Blackthorn or sloe (*Prunus spinosa*) is often there and this is the food plant of the brown hairstreak (*Thecla betulae*), the black hairstreak (*Strymonidia pruni*), and, in Europe, of the sloe hairstreak (*Nordmannia acaciae*). Curiously enough no European butterfly uses lime (*Tilia* spp.) as a principal food plant, although limewoods used to make dominant stands on rich fertile lowlands which were some of the first areas cleared by man.

Beechwoods

Climax communities of beech, like lime, do not have any associated butterfly species. A mature beechwood is devoid of vegetation on the woodland floor since the summer canopy is complete and interlocking, and does not allow sunlight to percolate down to the woodland floor. Beechwoods occur on chalky soil. However, close by there may be either an area which is being systematically degraded by the invasion of sycamore or an area of scrub invaded with chalk-loving plants. The latter habitat is one of the best places to study butterflies. In these open clearings there will be blues, coppers, browns and fritillaries.

Around the outside of a beechwood, or roving around the scrub will be the brimstone butterfly which changes its habitat preference as it gets older. In the summer and autumn it lives in the open looking for suitable nectar sources but when freshly out of hibernation it is eager to locate its food plants — the ordinary and the Mediterranean buckthorn (*Rhamnus* spp.), chalk-loving plants — found in the woods and scrub. In the woods the brimstone is thought to be the principal pollinator of primroses (*Primula vulgaris*) since it has a long tongue which effects cross-pollination. The other brimstone food plant is alder buckthorn (*Frangula alnus*) which is also found on limestone areas as well as on acid soils.

Close to beechwoods and on chalk grassland peppered with scrub bushes, the dark green fritillary may be seen. Like its other two large relatives which prefer denser scrub and woodland clearing, the high brown fritillary and the silver-washed fritillary (*Argynnis paphia*) use violets as their caterpillar food plants. There are at least a dozen fritillary species in Europe which use violets as food plants. Violets occur in several habitat types which explains why different fritillary species are found in meadows, light woodland, woodland clearings and along roadsides and paths.

Box, Juniper and Yew Scrub

On limestone areas, particularly on the Continent, box, juniper and yew may be present. The typical areas in which these three associated plant species occur are the flat limestone plateaux (*causses*) which are found up to 600 to 900 m altitude. Here the vegetation is sparse and occasionally the limestone rocks exhibit their characteristic pavement effect. This type of habitat also occurs in the Yorkshire National Park and in the Burren in western Ireland, some 1,600 km away. Surprisingly much of the habitat and the flora is virtually identical. The scenery is so uncannily alike that you could think you were in the other place.

However, the warmth of western Ireland cannot compete with southern France, where the intense heat and sunshine that butterflies like produces a much richer butterfly fauna. On these Continental *causses* there are often two associated plant species, box (*Buxus* spp.) and juniper

(*Juniperus* spp.). In England yew (*Taxus baccata*) makes up a third species which is now only rarely found in the presence of the other two. C.J. Smith's *The Ecology of the English Chalk* (1980) is thoroughly recommended as the interaction of all forms of wildlife are discussed. In a natural habitat, box and juniper are protector species for yew regeneration. When the yew matures the other two species die off, thus maintaining the climax yew community.

Yew produces noxious resinous substances which not only deter other plants from growing near to it but effectively keep plant-eating insects at bay. Box and juniper are very important in the lives of butterflies on the Continent. They are used as perch points for territorial behaviour and as resting posts for spending the night. None of the European butterflies uses box and juniper, however, as a food plant.

The species of butterfly with the greatest adaptations to life on these limestone *causses* belong to the Satyridae family; the grayling, the hermit (*Chazara briseis*), the black satyr (*Satyrus actaea*), and the false grayling (*Arethusana arethusa*). Clouded yellows (*Colias* spp.) and some of the nymphalids pass through on migration, stopping off at flower-rich sites rich in globe thistles (*Echinops ritra*). The blues and coppers have exploited the members of the pea family growing in the cracks in the rocks.

MAN-MADE HABITATS

Man-made habitats are defined here as all those non-natural habitats created by man; such as the multitude in the urban environment (churchyards, gardens, golf-courses, airports), forestry and hedgerows and man-managed coppice woodlands. It is interesting to note that butterflies are quick to colonise many an area of waste grassland and that some species actually prosper when man ceases to cultivate areas. In England the white admiral continues to prosper in the neglected coppice woodland, in Italy the southern festoon (*Zerynthia polyxena*) prospers in several mountain areas where birthwort (*Aristolochia* spp.) thrives after withdrawal of cultivation. In many areas in southern Europe this suckering plant is a vineyard pest. Even under natural conditions new habitats are created through fires and landscapes and in Italy the large blues (*Maculinea* spp.) and the iolas blue (*Iolana iolas*) have moved in fast and colonised these areas.

Coppice woodlands provide an essential habitat for the heath fritillary (*Mellicta athalia*) in south-east England. The traditional way of managing these sites is to cut small parcels of the trees down every 15 years; for example, this rotation is done for sweet chestnut (*Castanea sativa*). This opens up a glade which springs to life with wild flowers including the food plant of the heath fritillary, cow-wheat (*Melampyrum* spp.). With the random felling of different parcels of land, under different ownership, it provided a patchwork of suitable butterfly habitats that were efficiently exploited by the butterflies. The heath fritillary still has the capability of forming very large populations in a relatively small habitat.

The present-day problems of these butterfly populations come from three sources: many coppice woodlands have been neglected and allowed to become thicker and thicker thus shutting out any butterfly habitats; others have been grubbed out entirely; and finally, clear-felling of coppice woodlands is often practised. Here large areas of coppice are felled since the woods may be in only one ownership and it is more profitable to fell entire areas than have patchy felling. The significance of this change means that the butterflies can no longer move round the corner to another suitable open habitat when its own one has temporarily matured. The intimate association of the heath fritillary with its traditionally managed coppice-woodland habitats of small glades is now doomed — except where conservation bodies look after the habitat on nature reserves in the interest of the butterflies.

Forestry Plantations

In lowland areas forestry plantations are not rich places for butterflies, birds or wild plants. This is because the monoculture of trees severely limits the possible forms of wildlife. Mountainous areas are slightly better. However, the rides, fire breaks and the forest edges do have a diverse flora which has infiltrated the habitat. Original habitats try to assert themselves along rides or round the margins and with a little practise you can detect indicator species of the former habitat trying to push themselves into this man-made habitat. These 'weeds' in the forestry stands support much of the insect life but are subjected from time to time to aerial spraying to eliminate them. The Arran brown (*Erebia ligea*) is a forest butterfly in Scandinavia and prefers mixed woods with conifers and in favourable places can be abundant. Another species, the woodland brown (*Lopinga achine*), as its name suggests, likes wooded areas, either mixed conifers or clearings of hazel (*Corylus* spp.), hawthorn (*Crataegus* spp.) and elm (*Ulmus* spp.) in open forests. It is rare and restricted, however, in southern Scandinavia.

In a sense the rides can be looked upon as linear nature reserves cut through areas of uninteresting conifers, like motorway verges through a sea of intensive agricultural land. Some butterflies have benefited from these strips of semi-natural grassland. In Britain the Forestry Commission should rejoice in the burgeoning butterfly populations which have been induced quite inadvertently; the butterflies again demonstrating their keen powers of dispersal, exploration and colonisation of new habitats.

Before the ancient forests were cleared by man, there would have been hundreds of thousands of kilometres of woodland edge, if you added up the margins of each parcel of wood. As man cleared the forests the figure dwindled to a fraction of the total. Stands of new forestry blocks with their rides have dramatically increased the 'woodland-edge effect' and provided butterflies with suitable places for survival.

On the Continent where coniferisation of the uplands has also continued unabated — turning natural mountain pastures and rugged hillsides into unattractive stands of silent conifers — the butterflies abound along the foresters' tracks. The tall conifers provide plenty of shelter from prevailing winds and when the sunshine pours into the tracks the wild flowers bloom rapidly. I know several foresters' tracks in the Cévennes where almost 30 species of butterfly can be seen just along a track about 30 m long.

But what has this habitat got that makes it so butterfly-rich? Could you recreate this habitat back home? Surprisingly the track does not look all that outstanding except for its plant diversity. It is hemmed in by tall conifers, there is a trickle of water coming out of the bank on one side, dribbling down the track and going off on the other bank. There are overhanging branches of elm, briars (*Rosa* spp.) and each side of the track are luxuriant growths of hemp agrimony (*Eupatorium cannabinum*), mints (*Mentha* spp.), rose bay willowherb (*Epilobium* spp.), nettles (*Urtica* spp.) and mullein. The warm sheltered habitat with an abundance of wild flowers and ample damp patches would be difficult to recreate at home.

Water is more vital in butterfly habitats in southern Europe than in Britain where the Atlantic climate allows for ample moisture and high humidity. Without water the plants do not produce sufficient nectar for sustaining butterflies. Many more plants occur around water than away from it. And males need to imbibe essential nutrients for the manufacture of their pheromones.

The Camberwell Beauty (*Nymphalis antiopa*) is a typical butterfly of forested areas on the Continent. Its large form is clearly recognised in the spring after it comes out of hibernation, for it probably uses the hollow and split tree trunks in which to spend the winter. During the summer it joins the myriads of fritillaries and other nymphalids drinking nectar at the colourful scabious (*Knautia* spp.) and knapweed (*Centaurea* spp.) strewn corners.

Both the orange tip and the wood white (*Leptidea sinapis*) have expanded their ranges in Britain thanks largely to new man-made habitats to their liking in the form of forestry plantation rides. The wood white finds the rides attractive since its food plants, everlasting pea (*Lathyrus*) and birdsfoot-trefoil (*Lotus corniculatus*) occur there.

The forestry drainage ditches are important to butterflies like the orange tip since water-loving plants, such as the cuckoo flower (*Cardamines pratensis*), thrive in these conditions. The edge-effect — of plants growing around the margins of woods or along rides — is important to most butterfly species which live in forestry areas. The expansion of the orange tip in northern England may have also been due to subtle changes in the climate. A marked fall in the mean temperature of April over the last 20 years may have caused delay in emergence which would have been advantageous. Better weather later in the year would provide more flight periods for individuals to find each other. Being a springtime butterfly the orange tip has to be active in between the 'April showers' and sometimes the early April weather is not very kind to it. That is why they have evolved the strategy of early emergence of males so that courtship and mating can be accomplished in the minimum of time between the long spells of bad weather.

Hedgerows

Nearly all hedgerows are man-made, with thorny anti-stock species like hawthorn, blackthorn/sloe (*Prunus* spp.) and holly (*Ilex aquifolium*) often planted. Very few hedgerows were formed from an uncut part of the original forest. It is fortunate from the entomological point of view that hedgerows can accumulate more plant species as they become older; one extra woody species on average for every 100 years thus forming the basis of the technique of hedgerow-dating.

Hedgerows have accumulated a wide variety of butterfly species which are dependent upon the hedgerow habitat. Some species not only feed as caterpillars in the foliage but feed as adults on the profusion of wild plants which grow at the edge of the hedgerow. It was a simple move from the forest/woodland edge to the hedgerow edge. As one refuge was removed by man several butterflies made the successful exploratory flight to a similar one recently created. From a butterfly's point of view a hedgerow offers several different sub-habitats: sun-traps influenced by position and aspect; abundance of foliage of different ages and in different positions for caterpillar food plants; abundant leaf surfaces for sun basking; shade in and outside the hedge for those butterflies which are shade-loving; and old tree trunks as well as hollow ones, for hibernating butterflies.

But the majority of butterflies associated with hedgerows are sun-lovers, like the gatekeeper (*Pyronia* spp.), whose British species *tithonus* also has the appropriate common name of hedge brown. However, the three *Pyronia* butterfly species are not at all restricted to the hedgerow habitat. They occur in grassy areas, along woodland rides, dried up river beds and anywhere where there is an abundance of grasses and wild flowers for the caterpillars and adults to feed on respectively. Adults need an abundance of wild flowers, especially brambles in a hedgerow habitat, or scabious, hawkbits (*Leontodon* spp.) and wild clematis (*Clematis* spp.). One of their best habitats is rough marginal land overflowing with wild flowers, grasses and shrub trees adjacent to a hedgerow. Preferably the habitat should be a real hot spot, enclosed by trees or formed by strong contours in the land. This sort of habitat may be found amongst marginal forestry land (more on the Continent than in Britain where there is more pressure on space) as well as in deciduous woodland, but equally the butterflies find waste areas around towns and cities to their liking.

Other butterflies which have grass-feeding caterpillars, like the skippers and browns, can become abundant along the grassy margins of hedgerows — the Essex skipper and small skipper, the small heath and meadow brown (*Maniola jurtina*). The large skipper may be present where there are clearings and scrub. Other skippers found along hedgerows such as the *Pyrgus* grizzled skippers, the dingy and the mallow skippers (*Carcharodus alceae*) may be rather local in their distribution since they have less abundant non-grass food plants.

It is the interface between the hedgerow and the next habitat, for instance a roadside verge, which is often most important for hedgerow butterflies. A drainage ditch encourages the growth of moisture-loving plants which in turn attract butterflies like the orange tips (*Anthocharis* spp.) and the green-veined white (*Artogeia napi*). Wild crucifers enjoy the wet conditions of the ditch and these are eagerly sought after for oviposition sites by these members of the white family.

The brimstone and its southern European relation the cleopatra (*G. cleopatra*) are both hedgerow species which have a great woodland affinity. The brimstone goes on many patrolling flights along the hedgerow and will rest in vegetation or stop to feed on typically mauve-red flowers like thistles, periwinkle (*Vinca* spp.) or purple loosestrife (*Lythria purpurea*). Its wing's uncanny resemblance to an ivy leaf defies predators and entomologists alike in finding it, for it is thought to hibernate within ivy leaves. The importance of old timbers and decayed tree trunks in a hedgerow habitat cannot be overstressed.

Hedgerows are used by butterflies as corridors for movement across country. Unlike birds which use fixed visual objects as aids in their navigation, butterflies will sometimes use a hedgerow as a means of crossing the countryside. A tall hedge will arrest the movement of a butterfly and divert it along its length where it will sometimes find nectar sources and sheltered spots to its liking; all a butterfly-lover has need to do is sit and wait for the butterflies to come along. Some of these butterflies may be well-known migrants, others are butterflies which exhibit only local movements.

The species most likely to do this movement along boundaries are the clouded yellows, the nymphalids, small tortoiseshell (*Aglais urticae*), the peacock (*Inachis io*) and the red admiral (*Vanessa atalanta*). The last two species may establish territories along the hedge at particular places and be seen frequently at these places. The comma (*Polygonia c-album*) and painted lady are other nymphalid butterflies which also make territories along hedgerows and in secluded corners, although the latter species may be found in many other habitats such as gardens and coastal dunes. Many of the nymphalid butterflies lay their eggs on the perennial stinging nettle (*Urtica dioica*) which is typically a hedgerow species, or, like the painted lady, on thistle also found along hedgerows. The natural habitat for the perennial nettle is 'probably open woodland on peaty soils (fen carr)' but it has exploited many other habitats since then. There are about 100 species of insect including butterflies which are associated with nettles at least in Britain.

Walking alongside hedgerows disturbs butterflies, especially those that are holding tight to their little bits of territory. The wall butterfly (*Lasiommata megera*) is one which can be 'pushed' along its particular length of hedgerow many times. It flies off, settles, displays with wings open, is disturbed and flies off again only to repeat the behaviour several times again before returning to one of its former positions. When not behaving very territorially the wall butterflies can get so engrossed in drinking nectar from scabious that they become very approachable, particularly for photography. Normally they are one of the most nervous of butterflies to approach at close quarters. The speckled wood is also found along old hedgerows basking and holding territories just as they do in woodland glades. The speckled wood is more of a shade-loving butterfly than the wall which is a real sun-worshipper, basking for hours in the sun.

Loss of hedgerows has of course reduced the total hedgerow habitat available to butterflies. Populations have suffered and local extinctions occurred. It is thought that 45 per cent of the eggs of the brown hairstreak (*Thecla betulae*) can be lost if hedgerows are cut between September and April when the eggs are hibernating on the plants. The eggs are laid on new growth which is the first to be trimmed when a hedgerow is cut. Apart from man's activities the butterfly populations have to contend with bird and parasite depredations.

Gardens and Urban Habitats

Members of the Royal Sandwich Bay Golf Club in East Kent have a special Nature Conservancy leaflet alerting them to be careful of the rare wild plants growing on their course. The rough areas of golf-courses are very good places for wildlife and many a county or even national rarity has been found on them.

There are plenty of other habitats for butterflies and wild plants in urban and suburban areas: parks and gardens, cemeteries, churchyards, railway junctions and verges, refuse tips and waste areas. But the most important for butterflies is gardens. Together 'the garden habitat' is enormous and very varied.

Churchyards and cemeteries are very important places for butterflies, in fact several have been made into nature reserves. At present the results of a national survey of the wildlife of such places in Britain is still being analysed by the Botanical Society of the British Isles and the Women's Institute who organised it. With such a long list of wild plants that are surviving in such 'reservoir' sites in urban areas it is not surprising that butterflies have moved into these safe havens. The rigours of ploughing, herbiciding and insecticiding have generally been kept outside the churchyard wall. As so many churchyards were claimed originally from the countryside some may harbour relic species of plants.

Refuse tips offer an attractive habitat for butterflies, though an unattractive and relatively inaccessible place for lepidopterists to study. I have seen on my own local refuse tip seven species of butterfly flying on one June day, the skippers and nymphalids exploiting the wild plants as caterpillar food plants and nectar sources for adults.

Overgrown gardens may have stands of nettles, thistles, grasses; kitchen gardens are full of cultivated crucifers; whilst formal gardens are rich in butterfly bushes (*Buddleja* spp.), Michaelmas daisies and sedums. From a butterfly's point of view there are nectar-rich flowers all year round somewhere in town since they have open access to all gardens. Municipal gardens often offer a great variety of attractive flowers.

The kitchen garden has always been plagued with depredations from some pierid members of the white family of butterflies. They are so successful that even 40 years on from assailing them with organic

Figure 6.3   Butterflies in the garden

insecticides their caterpillars still completely defoliate some cabbage patches. (The inorganic poisons of pre-1940 were often more poisonous to man and beast than the present day organics.) Under intensive horticulture insects have a raw deal with the tonnes of insecticides applied to plants. Like frogs and toads, the cabbage butterflies are now more common in the urban environment than in the countryside. This is especially true for southern England where intensive agriculture has wiped out much woodland.

The common garden butterflies are those whose caterpillars eat either grasses, nettles or cabbages. Much encouragement is given these days to create a 'natural' garden; a garden full of wildlife. Where some people leave a garden as a wilderness (sometimes as an excuse for not gardening), others deliberately leave a garden to itself and practice minimal management, encouraging butterfly (or moth) food plants. Long grass, lady's smock (*Cardamine pratensis*), mignonette (*Reseda lutea*), garlic mustard (*Alliaria petiolata*), docks, (*Rumex* spp.), hawthorn and elm are worth promoting for caterpillar food plants; whilst fleabane (*Pulicaria dysenterica*), scabious, dandelions (*Taraxicum officinalis*), privet (*Ligustrum vulgare*) and valerian (*Valeriana officinalis*) are worth promoting for nectar sources. All these plants are native species to Britain without relying on introduced garden plants for butterflies.

Town and city gardens may be graced with butterflies, visiting on their exploratory journeys. Provided the lures are there the butterflies will eventually come. Migratory butterflies even frequent town gardens. Miriam Rothschild and Clive Farrell's book *The Butterfly Gardener* (1983) is fascinating to read for its pioneering work on garden design, recommended plant species and love of butterflies.

7 Butterflies and sunshine

Sombre tenant of the glade
Lover of the cooling shade
In nooks retiring wilt thou hide
Afraid to show thy 'speckled' pride

Joseph Merrin (1820–1904)

INTRODUCTION

Discussion has rarely been focused upon the very influential role of sunshine in the lives of butterflies. This chapter seeks to provide an overview of this association, after all, butterflies are creatures of sunshine and their gay colours are there to be seen and noted.

The importance of sunshine to butterflies is crucial. Without it they would be dead. It is their elixir of life. Their bright wing colours are enhanced by sunshine, they recognise each other by their different sexual colours and different absorption of ultra-violet light, they fly in it, they court in it and will readily mate in it (compare the relative ineffectiveness of matings under artificial light), their distribution is governed by it, their potential attack from parasites is influenced by it, their behaviour is governed by the amount and intensity of sunlight energy and light and, indirectly, the release of their plant foods (nectar) is determined by the amount of light.

As an example of the importance of sunshine and habitat the black hairstreak (*Strymonidia pruni*) has a specific habitat requirement of 'a network of sheltered sunny banks of blackthorn and glades within a woodland system'. Nowhere else are warm hollows and 'sunspots' so important as with the butterflies which live within the Arctic Circle. Many of the butterflies which live in Arctic conditions are black or have black spots to help them absorb the sun's radiant energy.

Sunshine then, is such an important factor to butterflies that it enters into many aspects of the biology and ecology of butterflies. Reference can be made to Chapters 5 (Coloration and Camouflage), 6 (Habitats) and 8 (Populations and Territories) for further information on involvement of sunshine in structural colours, keeping warm, warm habitats and sunny territorial patches.

The association of butterflies with sunshine has captured the hearts of numerous poets and authors. William Henry Hudson in his *Hampshire Days* (1903) described the woodland butterflies '. . . the purple emperor . . . and the silver-washed fritillary are seen at one spot playing about the bracken in some open sunlit space in the oak wood, opening their orange-red spotty wings on the broad vivid green fronds they produce a strikingly beautiful effect'.

The amount of sunshine that any habitat receives through the year controls the distribution of some butterfly species. Thus the relative paucity of butterfly species in, for instance, Scotland, as opposed to the south of France. Or one could compare Britain's 55 resident species with over 1,000 species in the tropical climate of the Malay Peninsula which is of comparable territorial size. Although the wood white (*Leptidea sinapis*) has experienced increased distribution of its range in northern England in recent years, its limit to further exploitation is the lack of enough sunshine for seeking mates and courtship in the crucial spring period. In detailed ecological studies carried out on this butterfly by Martin Warren, whilst doing his doctoral research at Cambridge University, the 'best' habitats for these butterflies were shady rides which had 170 and 230 mW/cm^2/a day of light. Other ecological factors are important too. It was found significant that the food plants, species of trefoil and vetch, should be of medium or large size and at least greater than 20 cm tall.

Quite a number of butterflies have caterpillars which bask in the sun (heath fritillary, *Mellicta athalia*; the Glanville fritillary, *Melitaea cinxia*; and the marsh fritillary, *Euphydryas aurinia*). The jet black caterpillars of the marsh fritillary really do absorb the sun's energy whilst basking since Keith Porter recorded their internal temperature between 35–37°C. Early instar gregarious caterpillars bask in the early spring sunshine whilst individual fully-grown caterpillars move to shadier places in order to reduce overheating and maintain their internal temperature at a maximum of 37°C. It is fascinating that sunshine has an effect not only on the sex ratio of the butterfly but on the synchronous attacks from the parasitic wasp (*Apanteles bignelli*). Relatively cold soil temperatures in the spring induce the parasites to hatch from their pupae almost too late to

Figure 7.1   Communal web of Glanville fritillary caterpillars

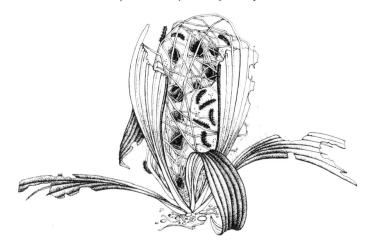

parasitise the butterfly caterpillars which are nearly fully-grown. Female caterpillars take a few extra days to develop and consequently they can all find themselves subject to attack from the newly-emerged parasites. Any quicker development would mean that the caterpillars might have escaped the depredations from the parasites.

It is interesting how vagaries in the weather can have an apparently significant effect on butterfly populations and their distribution. E.B. Ford reminds us that the pale clouded yellow (*Colias hyale*) can actually survive typical British winter temperatures of below 4°C. However, other climatic and biotic effects act on overwintering insects, such as damp and fungi. Some increase in the range of the white admiral (*Ladoga camilla*) is accredited to warm summers in the 1930s. Extensions in the range of the orange tip (*Anthocharis cardamines*) in northern England may be explained by relatively poor springs, in fact, due to a marked fall in the mean April temperature over the previous 20 years. Emergence of adults was delayed so that when the butterfly did fly there was warm weather suitable for survival and exploratory flights. For most species of butterfly the weather at the time the female is likely to mate and lay eggs is very crucial for the well-being of that species. Bad weather may radically affect its future.

Sunshine, when combined with lack of rain, aggravates drought conditions. The year of 1976 was remarkable in Britain for its drought and at least five species of butterfly suffered population declines — the dingy skipper (*Erynnis tages*), the common blue (*Polyommatus icarus*), the small copper (*Lycaena phlaeas*), the wall (*Lasiommatus megera*) and the ringlet (*Aphantopus hyperantus*). This effect was particularly relevant to Britain because of its normally wet Atlantic climate. In many areas of southern Europe drought conditions are a regular phenomenon since it does not rain significantly between April and October. The butterflies found in these regions are therefore well adapted to these hot, dry and very sunny habitats. In contrast, the wetter west coast of Britain is favoured particularly by the small pearl-bordered fritillary (*Boloria selene*) and the dark green fritillary (*Argynnis aglaja*); the caterpillars of the latter develop quicker in full sunlight.

Figure 7.2   Mallow skipper basking on spurge flowers

There is no doubt that butterflies can see in the ultra-violet (UV) since studies show that the wings of male and female absorb relatively different amounts of UV. Ordinary daylight contains masses of UV light and this is differentially absorbed on the petals of flowers. Our own eyes cannot see any of the UV light yet there is still plenty of it about even on bright cloudy days. That's why many butterfly species are active on bright overcast days; they do not have to have clear blue skies and scorching sunlight, though it does help. The 'honey-guides' on petals help butterflies to find nectar-rich food plants and in relieving the plants of their nectar butterflies contribute in cross-pollination. The guides would not be visible without the UV. The incredible co-evolutionary phenomenon of pseudo-copulation of some orchids by various solitary bee species is nowhere approached in finesse by any European butterflies. Cross-pollination of primroses (*Primula* spp.) by brimstones (*Gonepteryx rhamni*) is as close as we can get.

Butterflies which spend most of their lives in direct incident light face a formidable risk from desiccation. Softer bodied caterpillars have an even greater problem. However, they have both clearly made great adaptations to searing heat and low humidities, since butterflies and many of their caterpillars, scorn the oppressive heat of the midday sun and thrive in some of the sunniest and hottest places in Europe. They occur in vast numbers where man, who automatically controls his own body from overheating, can only tolerate the heat for short periods and has to find respite in the shade. Butterflies cope with these adverse conditions through the evolution of light colour variants and differences in their behaviour.

Two scorching hot habitats rich in butterfly species come to mind. The first and most numerous are the high altitude limestone *causses* so typical of the western areas of the Massif Central in France. These are calcareous regions with outcrops of rock which stretch for thousands of square kilometres. The sun and wind keep the calcareous rock a searing white which contributes to the countryside looking so bright and light coloured. Many of the satyrid butterflies living here assume a very pale coloration to blend in with their background. This has been described elsewhere as a 'white-out effect'.

The second area is around the red-soiled asphaltic wastes of Lac de Salagou near Clermont l'Herault in southern France (Herault). Here I have personally measured the temperature at ground level in full sun in early July as 57°C. One metre above the ground, and away from reflected heat, it is cooler at 37°C. Even so butterflies are flying actively and visiting flowers at ground level whilst humans flag. Similar temperatures are undoubtedly a feature during the summer months on the limestone *causses* or on other types of habitats such as open granite or micaschist rock or sandy areas like the dunes of the southern Camargue.

Swallowtails, migrant nymphalids, graylings, clouded yellows (*Colias* spp.) and black-veined whites (*Aporia crataegi*) are frequently found in these habitats under such severe conditions of heat and desiccation. They search out nectar from plants such as globe thistles (*Echinops ritro*) and St Barnaby's thistle (*Centaurea solstitialis*), whilst some seek out caterpillar food plants in the fennel (*Foeniculum vulgare*) and the many other species of thistles. Both the plants and butterflies have adaptations to these hot conditions, the plants with reduced surface area of leaves, the butterflies with pale forms to reflect heat.

Sunshine is what most butterflies thrive in but some can sense a change in the weather. Butterflies with a good weather sense are few but the ringlet is exceptional. It has strong powers of detecting a change for the worse in the weather. In anticipation of impending bad weather it will seek a secure resting site while it is still very bright. According to Henriksen and Kreutzer's observations in Scandinavia the butterflies show a great urgency in their mating drive prior to bad weather arriving, but if they show a rather 'unworried' flight good weather is assured for a while! The ringlet then is as good as honey-bees (*Apis mellifera*) at weather forecasting; their advanced warning is probably due to their detecting a fall in the air pressure.

The relative aspect of a habitat is of great importance to butterflies because the angle of incident sunshine determines the amount of warmth. How many times do we hear that a 'sheltered hollow' is a favourite haunt for butterflies, especially if it is south-facing. Groups of up to 20 silver-spotted skippers (*Hesperia comma*) have been recorded in Scandinavia in suitable habitats. Many of the blues favour south-facing sites throughout Europe, whether it is in southern England, Picardy, Dordogne or Cévennes of France or an alpine meadow. Several of the Arctic-living fritillaries and browns also like sheltered sunny hollows. 'Sun spots' are often sheltered hollows where butterflies gather and breed, sometimes in great numbers. On the mountainous coast of western Norway the northern clouded yellow (*Colias hecla*) concentrates at sun spots, which are peculiarly formed on some cloudy days when 'limited areas of approximately 100 m can receive more concentrated sunlight due to the mountain's physical effect on the formation of airstreams'. An active flier dependent on sunshine, it rests in vegetation as soon as the sun goes behind a cloud.

Butterflies change their habitats at different times of the day to regulate the effects on them of sunshine or wind, as in the Lapland fritillary (*Euphydras iduna*) which chooses south-west facing slopes in the afternoon, or selects different habitats according to altitude. The Arctic grayling, (*Oeneis bore*), lives at altitudes of about 1,000 m on the north-east side of the mountains where there are stony, flat mountain ridges or a flat, stone-covered plateaux with small grassy areas, preferably with steep mountain slopes to the west to lessen the effect of the wind. The very short bursts of sunshine frequently experienced within the Arctic Circle are sufficient for the sexes of the Arctic grayling to find each other and mate. They are 'heat and sun-lovers' in their northern Finland habitats and crawl into refuges in rocks and grass tufts as soon as bad weather comes. The polar fritillary (*Clossiana polaris*) also flies in bright sunshine and it too crawls into cracks during storms and bad weather.

Not all butterflies are sun-worshippers and these may prefer the dimmer light intensities of woodland margins or the understoreys and clearings of woods. In Arctic regions the daylength is severely limited and the amount of incident sunlight may be curtailed due to prolonged bad weather. Amongst the woodland butterflies there are many species which rely on the mottled effect of dappled light filtering through overhanging branches (e.g. speckled wood, *Pararge aegeria*), or prefer the cooler confines of woodland (e.g. great banded grayling, *Brintesia circe*, and wood white, *Leptidea sinapis*), whilst the brimstone flits between shady woodlands and open sunny waysides.

Butterflies orient themselves to the sun and much evidence can be seen of this in the field, either in the position they assume in relation to the sun's rays or the 'fidgeting' around immediately after landing. Butterflies which need as much sunlight energy as they can get may open their wings wide thus exposing as much of the surface area of their four wings as possible, or side on, with fore wings raised in the unique skipper fashion. In these cases this 'sun-bathing' behaviour is to maximise the beneficial effects of the sun's energy. In contrast, other butterfly species which habitually live in open sunny habitats, presumably like to minimise their exposure and may orientate away from it. During the morning it may be more critical to absorb the sun's energy, but at midday to minimise absorption. The shadow cast by an alighted butterfly can be controlled in some species by leaning over.

In the spring and autumn absorption of sunlight energy is more important to butterflies than in the summer, since overnight and early morning temperatures may be low. The springtime butterfly, the green hairstreak (*Callophrys rubi*) alights on rocks so that its wings are sideways on to the incident light. By doing this more surface area is available for absorption. The grayling (*Hipparchia semele*) also alights side on to the sun and it has the knack of leaning over sideways so as not to cast such a long shadow. This has a dual function, first, reducing the angle of incident light and second, decreasing the area of shadow as a defensive strategy.

In contrast there are those butterflies which align themselves parallel with the sun's rays. Some face towards the sun, others away. In the spring I have watched the comma (*Polygonia c-album*) facing away from the sun with only a short thin shadow to its front. I have also seen the speckled wood facing away from the sun, parallel with the rays, in an English wood in the spring.

The white-letter hairstreak (*Strymonidia w-album*) spends a great deal of time sitting around on leaves, more often in the shade, high up in a tree; I have seen them in black mulberry (*Morus nigra*) in southern France where they feed on the juice of the fruit. If the sun reaches their resting spots they align themselves sideways to the sun's rays. The purple hairstreak (*Quercusia quercus*) also spends much time resting on leaves and, judging from my photographs, it casts a long shadow over the leaves (themselves often dark, e.g. *Ulmus*) when they align side on to the sun.

Although butterflies are cold-blooded, they still have to adjust their internal temperature to maintain their metabolic rate. Magnus (1958) noted that the silver-washed fritillary (*Argynnis paphia*) maintains an internal temperature of 34°C by adjusting the position of its wings so as to catch a smaller or a greater proportion of the radiation from the sun. Feeding at attractive flowering plants in clearings and margins this butterfly is always in and out of sunshine which facilitates temperature regulation.

Resting on flowers with wings outstretched certainly does not mean that the butterfly is necessarily directly using the sun as a heating agent. Some may open their wings for advertisement, for mates and rivals, to deter predators or for defence. Two species rest with wings reflexed around flowers, the marbled white (*Melanargia galathea*) and the dingy skipper (*Erynnis tages*). Marbled whites often rest for long periods in the sun with their wings spread out, sometimes reflexed below their bodies and round the flower. They appear dead and can be picked up from the flower with a

Figure 7.3   White-letter hairstreak resting on leaf

little skill. The marbled white has the best of both worlds since the white areas reflect the heat and the black areas absorb the sunlight energy. In northern latitudes black colours may be more useful to the butterfly, particularly with the dark *Erebia* species (see Chapter 5).

The reflexed attitude of the dingy skipper is probably evolved more for camouflage than for photo-absorption since it roosts like this on flowers and with its dismal colours is not likely to be seen by predators. It is the only British skipper which engages in this untypical skipper manner of repose.

There are many butterflies which always rest with their wings closed. Several of these are species which abound in the open on hill tops and mountain tops, and whose caterpillars feed on the grasses which dominate many a high mountain pasture or craggy slope. The rock grayling (*Hipparchia alcyone*) flies to one place after another if disturbed. It sometimes alights side on to the sun, or in the shade, but more often it aligns itself parallel to the sun's rays and drops its fore wings in a lower position between its hind wings. By doing this it effectively casts only a thin fine shadow of reduced length. This is ideal for camouflage. This is combined with a quick 'set-down' reaction to confuse and disorientate the pursuing predator.

Orientation is crucial to butterflies seeking places to sleep overnight. In meadows the blues settle down to a night head-down towards the top of grass stems. Other larger species go to sleep at the top of a tree facing the last few rays of the setting sun, but they will be in the wrong place for the morning sun. I have recorded the scarce swallowtail (*Iphiclides podalirius*) moving around to the east just before sunrise. They roost in olive trees (*Olea europea*) in southern France. Both the silver-washed and the high brown fritillary (*Argynnis adippe*) also use trees as roost sites overnight. I have also seen blue-spot hairstreaks (*Strymonidia spini*) roosting at the top of juniper bushes (*Juniperus* spp.) and white-letter hairstreaks roosting in black mulberry.

We have seen from Chapter 4 that there are very few tree species which support the caterpillars of butterflies. However, trees, together with the labyrinth of sunny glades, margins and speckled rides are vitally important for the spatial relationships of butterflies. The behaviour, territory establishment, courtship and mating of many butterflies is dependent upon this habitat arrangement. Few lepidopterists have bothered to sit in the canopy of woodland trees to study the habits of butterflies which live in full sunshine on the tree tops. Canopy platforms are essential, if luxurious, for the study of butterflies in this important sunny arena, just as they are in the tropical rainforests, where many more species are found high above than in the dark forests below. There are, though, many more butterflies which frequent lower levels away from woods and next time you sit in a flowery meadow surrounded by colourful cold-blooded butterflies, remember their dependence upon the sun whilst they dazzle you with their brilliant colours.

8 Populations and territories

... This plot of orchard-ground is ours;
My trees they are, my sister's flowers;
Here rest your wings when they are weary;
Here lodge as in a sanctuary!

William Wordsworth (1770–1850) *To a Butterfly*

INTRODUCTION

Many butterflies exhibit strong territorial behaviour and this is always played out in various types of habitats or parts of habitats which can be precisely defined. The nature of their territorial behaviour is a function of the spatial relationship of that habitat, the juxtaposition of the flowering herbs and trees, the amount of space and, of course, the amount and intensity of sunshine and shade.

This chapter deals first with butterfly populations generally, illustrating how numerous butterflies can be in certain habitats, then this is followed by an appreciation of butterflies' territories. What we find is that we really do not know much about the make up of butterfly populations and precious little about butterfly territories. What knowledge we do have is gleaned from the diligent observations of a few people and evidence from mark and recapture experiments.

If you come across a population of butterflies in the wild you must ask yourself whether the butterflies are there because this is where they grew up as caterpillars (i.e. are their caterpillar food plants present?), or whether the butterflies are there because they have already dispersed from their birth-habitat and have taken up station in an area rich in adult food plants where they might find a mate. Some butterfly species never move out of the habitat in which they grew up; whilst others move out immediately and set up temporary territories for the sole reason of seeking a mate.

Populations

Insects are the most successful animals on earth; butterflies are no exception. It is a characteristic of butterflies that they can sometimes be extremely abundant in very small habitats. If the conditions are right (aspect, warmth, food plants, light/shade) it is often surprising to lepidopterists how many numbers of butterflies of the same species may be contained in such a tiny area (see Table 8.1). The maximum number that any defined area will accommodate comfortably is called the carrying capacity but this can vary. Unfortunately habitats always change, grasslands change to scrub, scrub areas with intervening meadows are soon replaced with more scrub; so the success of butterfly populations is under the influence of natural change or plant succession. Exploitation of some man-made and man-managed habitats, like grass verges, arrests the plant succession and presents a more stable habitat which has been successfully exploited by hesperid and satyrid butterflies.

On the other hand some butterflies do not have any defined territory and may be migratory. Many of the pierids, such as the clouded yellows (*Colias* spp.) and black-veined white (*Aporia crataegi*), may be exceedingly abundant and exist over a very large area. I saw the whole region around the Massif of Mt Aigoual and the Causse de Blandas (both in the Herault *département* of France) thick with black-veined whites in June 1982. So many butterflies were spread over so many square kilometres that it led me to believe that their population was several million.

There are some well proven methods for estimating the total population of butterflies in a habitat and these have been well set out in Sir Richard Southwood's book on *Ecological Methods* (1966). One of the simplest ways of estimating butterfly populations is by mark and recapture; the proportion of specimens recaptured on subsequent days after marking gives an indication of the total population present. Ideally it is best to find a 'closed' habitat where no butterflies are entering the arena and none are leaving. Hopefully, you wish to sample a static population with no external influence, but in reality it is often impossible to find a 'closed' habitat. Births and deaths of butterflies also upset any population assessment and must be allowed for. However, some useful tit-bits of information can be gleaned from mark and recapture methods, such as average and maximum length of life of butterflies, and whether species are prone to move out of the area they were born in.

Islands represent an opportunity for lepidopterists to study butterfly populations that may better approach 'closed' populations. Professor Dowdeswell and Ronald Fisher first studied moth populations on the island of Cara in south-west Scotland but later turned to the small island of Tean (0.8 km long by 0.4 km wide) in the Isles of Scilly. Here they used mark and recapture methods on the meadow brown (*Maniola jurtina*) and recorded populations of 15,000, 3,000 and 500 individuals in three of their sample areas. On the neighbouring island of St Helen's, their estimates suggested a population size of 15,000 to 20,000 butterflies.

Table 8.1 The population structure of UK butterflies and minimum area from which a viable colony has been recorded. It is interesting to note that 26 species of butterfly can survive in habitats up to 2 ha in size. The large number of species with unknown areas for populations emphasises the need for further ecological research. This is a compilation from many sources taken from Jeremy Thomas's chapter on conservation of butterflies in *The Biology of Butterflies* and reproduced here, with slight modifications, by courtesy of The Royal Entomological Society of London. (*See opposite*)

Minimum Breeding Area (ha)	Closed Populations						Unknown area populations	Open or migratory populations
	0.5–1	1–2	2–5	5–10	10–50	>50		
	Essex skipper *T. lineola*	Lulworth skipper *T. acteon*	marsh fritillary *E. aurinia*	small pearl-bordered fritillary *B. selene*	swallowtail *P. machaon*	purple emperor *A. iris*	chequered skipper *C. palaemon*	holly blue *C. argiolus*
	small skipper *T. sylvestris*	dingy skipper *E. tages*	Glanville fritillary *M. cinxia*	pearl-bordered fritillary *B. euphrosyne*	brown hairstreak *T. betulae*		northern brown argus *A. artaxerxes*	comma *P. c-album*
	silver-spotted skipper *H. comma*	grizzled skipper *P. malvae*			large copper *L. dispar*		dark green fritillary *A. aglaja*	orange tip *A. cardamines*
	large skipper *O. venata*	wood white *L. sinapis*			white admiral *L. camilla*		high brown fritillary *A. adippe*	green-veined white *A. napi*
	purple hairstreak *Q. quercus*	green hairstreak *C. rubi*					silver-washed fritillary *A. paphia*	small white *P. rapae*
	black hairstreak *S. pruni*	small copper *L. phlaeas*					speckled wood *P. aegeria*	large white *P. brassicae*
	white-letter hairstreak *S. w-album*	brown argus *A. agestis*					wall *L. megera*	small tortoiseshell *A. urticae*
	small blue *C. minimus*	common blue *P. icarus*					mountain ringlet *E. epiphron*	peacock *I. io*
	silver-studded blue *P. argus*	adonis blue *L. bellargus*					Scotch argus *E. aethiops*	large tortoiseshell *N. polychloros*
	chalkhill blue *L. coridon*	large blue *M. arion*					large heath *C. tullia*	red admiral *V. atalanta*
	Duke of Burgundy fritillary *H. lucina*	grayling *H. semele*					gatekeeper *P. tithonus*	painted lady *C. cardui*
	heath fritillary *M. athalia*						ringlet *A. hyperantus*	clouded yellow *C. croceus*
	small heath *C. pamphilus*							
	meadow brown *M. jurtina*							
	marbled white *M. galathea*							
Total	15	11	2	2	4	1	12	12

87

Another factor which affects the study of populations is that butterfly populations fluctuate from year to year, and in some cases, there may be some long-term fluctuations over several decades (e.g. the comma, *Polygonia c-album*). One particular study by Dowdeswell showed how the meadow brown could fluctuate over several years by more than a factor of three. The 7 ha chalk downland site he found near Andover in Hampshire was effectively closed by dense deciduous woodland and, over several years, the populations of meadow browns fluctuated there from 3,000 to 10,000 insects.

Woodland butterflies offer interesting possibilities for population studies since they are sometimes confined to clearings and rides. Dietrich Magnus, working with silver-washed fritillaries (*Argynnis paphia*), marked 1,320 individuals (762 males, 558 females) and stated that this represented approximately a fifth of the whole population of his wooded valley under study in southern Germany — in other words a population of about 6,600. It would be interesting to see if this particular valley still sports this wonderful butterfly in such profusion 30 years after Magnus worked there.

Britain's rarest and most endangered resident species, the heath fritillary (*Mellicta athalia*), is a woodland species which is being intensively studied in its last major locality in Britain. Of 25 colonies remaining in the Blean woods, near Canterbury, Kent, 21 are small with populations of less than 200 on peak days of emergence. It is most unlikely that population sizes of this level are high enough to sustain this species indefinitely. However, the species does have the advantage that it can colonise local new areas provided its food plant is present.

Some butterflies become more and more restricted in their distribution and attempts have been made at estimating the total population in the country. The purple emperor (*Apatura iris*) is the best example in Britain. By finding out exactly how many individuals there are left some sort of conservation strategy can (hopefully) be drawn up, or, the information could then be used to classify the species as sufficiently endangered to join a list of protected species. T.S. Robertson perused the previous population estimation of Heslop for the purple emperor, took into consideration the massive loss of deciduous woodland from the countryside and formulated the estimate that 'the adult population for the whole country lies between 2,000 and 200,000'. That was in 1980. The hundred fold difference in figures was accounted for by ordinary annual fluctuations — a much larger fluctuation than in the silver-washed fritillary. Robertson admitted that the estimate is based on some highly questionable approximations and assumptions.

Another woodland butterfly, the wood white (*Leptidea sinapis*) was the subject of a Cambridge ecological survey by Martin Warren. He also demonstrated fluctuations in two populations at Yardley Chase in Northamptonshire, the largest of which declined from 3,600 individuals to 1,300 from 1978 to 1979. He noted too, that the carrying capacity of the rides would change as they mature.

The blues are both attractive and numerous and have received a fair amount of attention on their populations. Perhaps the largest population of blues is recorded for the adonis blue (*Lysandra bellargus*) whose population in one locality in Dorset in 1982 was estimated to be 60,000 adults. It had risen sharply from under 50 in 1977 but declines can be

Figure 8.1   Male wood white 'mud-puddling'

equally steep, often, regrettably leading to extinctions. The chalkhill blue (*Lysandra coridon*) may also be very numerous in a small area. It has been estimated that a medium-sized colony in Wiltshire contained about 18,000 adults in 2 ha and another in Kent had 5,000 males in 1 ha. Populations of many of the blues, it would seem, vary in their population size each year. The brown argus has been estimated up to 700 per colony.

Browns, too, can be very numerous. One has always seen large populations of marbled whites (*Melanargia galathea*) in relatively small areas. Even today, along old railway lines, forestry rides and on the Downs, the butterfly can be surprisingly numerous. One such population in Sussex was estimated by mark and recapture methods to have over a thousand adults in an area of 45,000 sq m of downland. The mountain ringlet (*Erebia epiphron*) has also been shown to have large populations of up to 9,000 individuals in Britain. In a mainland site for the meadow brown at Monks Wood populations of 500 to 100 have been recorded for a 4.2 ha field.

The more butterfly species become restricted in their distribution the more the last of their populations seem to be intensively studied. Some species, in their better localities, are down to their last hundred or so individuals. The situation may look quite grim. Of the grayling (*Hipparchia semele*), 'averaged sized' colonies in Devon are discussed by John Heath and colleagues as having a total emergence of 150. In places on the Continent the habitat of the grayling is so large that it is impossible to draw the line between one colony and the next. The butterflies exist, sometimes thinly, over a whole region. The small pearl-bordered fritillary (*Clossiana selene*) in an 'average' sized colony might have a total of 200 individuals.

In 1961 populations of the large heath (*Coenonympha tullia*) in Wales were estimated to be in the range of 1,000 to 2,000 adults. Population studies on the small heath (*Coenonympha pamphilus*) and of the small skipper (*Thymelicus sylvestris*) would prove to be interesting since they both tend to be abundant along roadsides, ditches and in grasslands.

Populations of butterflies fluctuate through the spring and summer season as generations die out and new ones flourish. A method for assessing the relative abundance of butterflies has been pioneered by Ernest Pollard at the Monks Wood Experimental Station. With his team of about 80 amateur recorders in Britain, a system of walking regular routes each week and recording the numbers of each butterfly species seen, he has been able to learn much about butterfly abundance. This is dealt with in detail in Chapter 10.

Territorial Behaviour

Several butterfly species exhibit territorial behaviour, some more than others, and most families of butterflies in Europe have good examples.

The hesperids show a high degree of keeping within their habitats. They are generally not noted for any local movement or migration and one might expect them to have evolved some sort of territorial behaviour to cope with high levels of interaction here. They are certainly extremely active little butterflies and the often-used description of being 'pugnacious' suits them well. They are agile and skilled fliers that go on reconnaissance missions to intercept others who penetrate their air-space (members of the same species, other butterfly species and insects like true flies, bees and wasps) and they also use their skill to track down mates, though little thoughtful quantitative work seems to have been done on this.

Butterflies like the green hairstreak (*Callophrys rubi*) and the purple hairstreak (*Quercusia quercus*) aggregate in suitable habitats (warm sheltered corners or around scrub trees, respectively). Here they are, metaphorically, always stumbling over themselves and therefore indulging in a high degree of interaction with members of each sex. They must have some sort of adaptation to alleviate any wasted energy in their tireless pursuits. The great swirls of single species butterflies which whirl round these habitats may well be involved in complex pheromone activity. From an observer's point of view there does not always seem to be any special purpose to these movements and one is tempted to suggest that this may be the closest that butterflies come to 'playing'.

Some of the swallowtails are extremely territorial whilst others appear not to show any territoriality. This does not mean that they do not have any territorial behaviour. The chances are that they have never been investigated.

The swallowtail family have species which have either open or closed habitats. The southern festoon (*Zerynthia polyxena*) is a feeble flier and lives in closed habitats with its caterpillar food plants. It does not seem to be territorial. Large populations of the apollo butterflies (*Parnassius apollo*) are found in small areas but they only seem to be present because of the abundance of adult food plants such as thistles which abound close to water sources.

The migrant swallowtails show great territoriality. *Papilio machaon* is the kind of butterfly which has a 'beat' — a large area around which it repeatedly flies. If you watch these butterflies in certain habitats it is the same butterfly which comes round again and again. Is it patrolling an area where it has found suitable nectar-rich food plants, or is it looking for a mate?

The scarce swallowtail (*Iphiclides podalirius*) is by far the most prestigious of the territory-holding swallowtails, and it is a species on which I have carried out research in the Cévennes. During the summer months the butterflies take up 'station' alongside buildings (the butterfly is strongly associated with man and his buildings) and continually fly a 'beat'. The patrolling behaviour involves a great deal of gliding, at which the scarce swallowtail is particularly expert. One flap of the wings is sufficient to glide 10 m along the side of a house, do a 180° turn and return to the start. If other scarce swallowtails are seen nearby (their white colours are clearly very obvious to patrolling butterflies) they immediately accelerate to intercept the potential intruder and give chase. Sometimes five or six butterflies will be involved in the fray. *I. podalirius* may become very damaged in its short life of three weeks in its efforts to maintain its territory and perch points, for it chooses particularly advantageous high spots on the tops of bushes on which to rest and to mount sallies against other insects.

Many of the pierids, like the orange tip (*Anthocharis cardamines*), the large white (*Pieris brassicae*) and the small white (*Pieris rapae*) demonstrate the 'edge-effect'; that is, patrolling the edges of woods along hedgerows, ditches and paths. In many cases they are physically guided along these avenues by the nature of the terrain; in some cases their movement, if migratory, is only in one direction, but in yet other cases, some of the butterflies may make a circuit. This is particularly so for the pale clouded yellow (*Colias hyale*). I have seen it going round and round in an old cereal field blossoming with wild flowers. It had become fixed on the particular colour of tall melilot (*Melilota altissima*) to which it was attracted — the colours of the flowers and the wings being very similar. Other pale clouded yellows became attracted to the melilot colours and thus joined the fray of interested adults.

A very interesting phenomenon has been witnessed by Henriksen and Kreutzer in Scandinavia. They found that the pale Arctic clouded yellow (*Colias nastes*) sometimes has 'rendez-vous' areas where all the newly-hatched butterflies aggregate from surrounding areas. For this species, which is rare south of the Arctic Circle, this characteristic must surely have been evolved to heighten the chances of matings in these austere regions where suitable weather for seek and find behaviour, courtship and matings is infrequent. In any case the right biotopes (flowery or scrubby rocky marshes and slopes) for these butterflies are few and far between as well. Therefore an arena for courtship interactions would be a logical evolutionary device for getting mated as soon as possible in the limited good weather available.

Amongst the nymphalids the Camberwell Beauty (*Nymphalis antiopa*) takes up station around large stands of willows where it has suitable food plants. Individuals have favourite leaves, tree trunks and fallen logs, in direct sunlight, where they return time and again for resting or maintaining their especially good 'hot-spots'. The two-tailed pasha (*Charaxes jasius*) does the same sort of thing but it is a much more powerful flier. It tends to have a larger area of beat than that of the Camberwell Beauty.

Silver-washed fritillaries may be very common along rides with plenty of nectar-giving flowers and sunshine but according to the studies of Magnus the males do not lay claim to a territory. Such large and distinctive butterflies do a lot of flying and one may see the males diving repeatedly under the females from behind, whilst flying at great speed, but this is all done in a habitat where presumably matings and intra-sex interactions are successful without establishing 'peck-orders' or rights over food plants or sunspots. Henriksen and Kreutzer observed in Scandinavia that several silver-washed fritillaries may co-exist in the same forest clearing, something that I can support also for the Massif Central in France. They transposed five females 'several kilometres' away from their original habitat and all but one made their way back. Although this butterfly does not apparently show any territoriality it seems to have a 'feeling' for its ideal 'behaviour arenas' within a forest or plantation and certainly does have an elaborate courtship ritual.

Males of the white admiral (*Ladoga camilla*) are strongly territorial. They assemble around large trees and sunny corners of clearings where they intercept passing females. Mated females disregard the advances of males and continue to go about their lives of nectar-feeding and egg-laying. It is not unusual to find a sunny corner where six or so of these beautiful woodland butterflies aggregate round a clump of bramble blossom.

The small tortoiseshell (*Aglais urticae*) is similarly territorial. Robin Baker studied this species and found that males on average establish two

Figure 8.2   White admirals make an excellent species of butterfly to study in their favourite corners of the wood

territories each day, mainly for the purpose of finding females. Establishment of territories usually began about noon and could last until roosting time. Territories were often in sunny positions with stinging nettles, against a wall or hedge and butterflies would hold them for about 90 minutes. This is very similar to the red admiral (*Vanessa atalanta*) which likes to defend its territories along hedgerows from special leaf perchpoints.

Purple emperors are well known for choosing prominent trees for the establishment of their territories. Males tend to keep to the highest branches and the females may be seen a little further down. According to Heslop some of the butterflies are only active for ten minutes in every ten hours of daylight, so that a lot of patience is needed to make observations. However, many people are afforded the opportunity of seeing the purple emperor at close quarters without too much trouble. If you are fortunate, it may 'swoop like a peregrine' to bright objects (even shiny cars) and to suck the juices from decaying carcases and animal dung. The poplar admiral (*Ladoga populi*) also appears curious and will come down to investigate people or their shiny cars.

The Lycaenidae, like the Hesperidae, are small butterflies which tend to have localised populations. Most are non-migratory and are mostly confined to a small habitat but there are some important exceptions. The territorial behaviour of the common blue (*Polyommatus icarus*) has been studied intensively by Lennart Lundgren in Sweden. He noticed how the males tear off after other butterflies (males and females of several species) and that it was not unusual for them to have a chase of more than 25 m. With the use of dummies he showed that males are attracted to their own bright colours, and even to those of other closely related butterflies. The bright colours appear to be primarily for other males not for female recognition of males. Douwes working with the scarce copper (*Heodes virgaureae*) eloquently described the way in which these butterflies maintain parts of their territories as 'intense traffic routes'. These were areas where two or more suitable habitats converged, sunspots and corners of rides and tracks and where there were plenty of flowers. The northern brown argus (*Aricia artaxerxes*) is also territorial. The males form territories, often away from their food plants, and use these as areas from which, or in which, to seek mates. The brown argus (*A. agestis*) is also thought to do the same, after all it is a very closely related species.

Figure 8.3   Male purple emperor imbibing juices from a fox dropping

Amongst the browns there are some excellent examples of territorial behaviour, especially with the speckled wood (*Pararge aegeria*) on which N.B. Davies did his classic work in an Oxfordshire wood, and the wall brown (*Lasiommata megera*) which has been investigated by Roger Dennis. Both these butterflies are perchers and patrollers, individuals of *aegeria* may be at any one time perching in sunny clearings or patrolling the canopy. The action of *megera* continually being pushed along a track, perching on rocky outcrops, bare earth and the like, is well known to walkers. One perching *megera* was seen to go on 27 'sorties' in 45 minutes and 11 of these were just exploratory inspection flights, not against other butterflies. There was much interchange of territories too, between males. In their patrolling behaviour it was interesting to note that up to three males may patrol the same beat — in this case a 100 m stretch of fenced path.

9 Migration

White butterflies in the air;
White daisies prank the ground.
The cherry and hoary pear
Scatter their snow around.

Robert Bridges (1844–1930) *Spring goeth all in white*

INTRODUCTION

In 1986 we still do not have all the explanations for butterfly migration. The simple questions about how, when, where and why have not been fully answered. This is despite a century of intensive study on the phenomenon of migration. A lot of quantitative information on the migratory movements of butterflies in Britain were amassed and published by C.B. Williams, T. Dannreuther and R.A. French in the 1950s and 1960s. Earlier this century Hans Blunck contributed much useful work on migrating butterflies whilst working in the north of Germany and today both Ulf Eitschberger and H. Roer keep up the tradition with the study of migration in Germany.

Britain has always led the world in having so many interested naturalists, whether they were eccentric Victorian or Edwardian collectors, or the vast array of today's amateur naturalists. The contributions made to the study of migration by the amateur recorders mobilised over the last 20 years by the Monks Wood Experimental Station is immense. Such an efficient recording system does not occur anywhere else in Europe or in the United States. Other recording schemes exist in Europe but the network of recorders is not so extensive. Special mention must also be made of the enthusiastic work of R.F. Bretherton and Michael Chalmers-Hunt in annually collating and publishing the data. Robin Baker's *Animal Migration* (1978) is such a definitive compilation that it is not likely to be surpassed.

There is no doubt that the migrations of butterflies today are nothing like those of the past. Even the migration of clouded yellows (*Colias* spp.) through western Europe in 1983 did not exceed that of 1947. A particularly colourful description of masses of large whites seen in France, at Calais in 1540, recorded:

'. . . the 9 of July, there was a sene at Calleys an innumerable swarme of whit buttarflye e somine out of the north-este and flyinge south-eastwarde, so thicke as flakes of snowe, that men being shutynge in Saint Petar's filde without the towne of Calleys cowld not se the towne of the cloke in the afternone, they flewe so highe and so thicke!'

Most of the European butterflies which are called migrants are technically not, since in the strict sense of the definition a migrant is one which moves to and from one place, often along well-defined routes. The definition is more applicable to birds than butterflies. Only a few butterfly species attempt a return migration, and this never takes them to their original source; they are killed off by the cold autumn. Ford mentions the monarch (*Danaus plexippus*) as 'a noted migrant' but it should be called a vagrant. Butterflies set off as emigrants (i.e. going away from) and arrive as immigrants (i.e. coming in to). In the popular sense species like clouded yellows are regarded as migrants, though technically they are emigrants or immigrants.

LIFETIME TRACKS

Keeping track of butterflies for the rest of their lives after they have emerged is the main obstacle to our further understanding of their way of life. Baker calls this path the 'lifetime track' which is so difficult to assess for any species. Marking butterflies is the best way of obtaining at least some idea of their movements but the chances of finding them again are always slight. The larger the animal the greater the chance of finding it; so with mute swans the return may be 90 per cent, with passerine birds less than 5 per cent and with frail insects less than 1 per cent. Dead insects are quickly eaten by other insects and disappear without trace.

As in population studies of butterflies in closed habitats the wings can be easily marked or painted so as to number or assign a batch number. Or the caterpillars can be fed on a dye which eventually stains the adult's eggs. Large numbers of the butterfly are needed so it may be more convenient to breed the species. This is what Meder did in northern Germany in the 1920s with three *Pieris* species, when he marked 4,000 to 5,000 individuals. Effective publicity requesting specimens gained him an extraordinarily high return of 850, or a sixth of the total marked. These marking experiments have been performed all too rarely and we rely on Roer's tagging experiments in Germany for the fact that the furthest a butterfly has been marked and recaptured in Europe is 95 km from Bonn to north-west of Dusseldorf for a large white (*Pieris brassicae*).

Quantitative evidence that butterflies arrive from far away places is incredibly scant. Where exactly have the red admirals (*Vanessa atalanta*) and painted ladies (*Cynthia cardui*) that adorn the asters and buddleia come from? Is it 300 km or 1,000 km away? What we learn from the widespread and much researched large white is that it can cover 10 km a day (sometimes helped by the wind) and in a generation these butterflies may cover 400 km. Naturalists have followed them on foot and by car to estimate speed and note direction, but their erratic flight (as captured in Robert Graves's poem, *Flying Crooked*, about the cabbage white: 'his honest idiocy of flight') causes much frustration. The small tortoiseshell (*Aglais urticae*) is an interesting species since some populations are sedentary, whilst others are migratory. On the mountain-top grasslands of the Apennines in Italy small tortoiseshells show some degree of migratory behaviour. In Britain small tortoiseshells are mostly sedentary but some are found in mid-Channel or flying over the North Sea.

We rely on one classic experiment, skilfully devised by Bernard Kettlewell in 1961, for evidence that one moth at least, the migratory pyralid (*Nomophila noctuella*), may well cover a distance of about 2,400 km during its short life. Kettlewell knew that an atomic bomb was due to be tested in the Sahara Desert at the time when migrants might be departing. After alerting lepidopterists in Europe to be on the look out for ordinary migrant insects one 'hot' specimen eventually turned up in Britain. It was found to have a minute radioactive particle on its body which it was thought to have picked up before leaving Africa. If a moth with a wingspan of only 28 mm can cover this distance, it might be thought that a much larger and more powerful butterfly could easily fly the distance. However, there is probably a distinct advantage in being small! Robin Baker believes that a butterfly like the small white (*Pieris rapae*) can cover 100 to 200 km over its lifetime track. He cites in support the fact that this species managed to colonise Australia, east to west, in three years after it was introduced to Melbourne in 1939. To do this the butterfly would have covered about 4,000 km in a maximum of 25 generations.

WHICH SPECIES MIGRATE?

There are species which are strongly migratory, other which are definitely not migratory, and yet others which have just a few individuals of their populations which are migratory. A similar state of affairs occurs in birds. As examples, the painted lady is a strongly migratory butterfly, the wood white (*Leptidea sinapis*) is a sedentary non-migratory butterfly and the speckled wood (*Pararge aegeria*) is one where only a few individual females emigrate out of their woodland habitats.

The majority of butterflies are non-migratory, especially amongst the skippers, browns and fritillaries. Individuals of these non-migratory species do turn up away from their normal haunts and this is generally seen as wandering or exploratory movements. Such butterflies may also be called vagrants. For example the Camberwell Beauty (*Nymphalis antiopa*) is a wandering species and may be found well away from its forest edge and riverside breeding areas, even in city squares in Denmark. The green underside blue (*Glaucopsyche alexis*) is also a great wanderer. Variation within the species occurs in the swallowtail (*Papilio machaon*) which, in Britain, is regarded as non-migratory, yet on the Continent is a common vagrant.

The distinction must be drawn between migration and local movement. Migration implies that the insect moves well away from one area to another, often hundreds of kilometres away. Local movement is the movement of butterflies from one local area to another, often over a kilometre or two. There are few examples of the latter, but it is quite possible to see how a local movement may have given rise to migration over millions of years. Essentially there is probably no fine division between the two phenomena.

The grayling (*Hipparchia semele*) in southern Europe is a good example demonstrating local movement. Over many years I have witnessed this butterfly streaming off the mountains in the Basse-Cévennes in the autumn, from the high altitude plateaux down into the valleys below. It occurs in about two out of every five years and when it does it is a very impressive event over a very wide front — as much as about 10 km. What I am sure happens is that the spring and summer months support such a good crop of grasses on the mountain tops (on granite, micaschist and limestone) that the late summer populations of the grayling increase enormously. This results in thousands of graylings streaming off the hills in late summer and early September. If you sit down across the track of the advancing butterflies they fly past you at the rate of about 10 every five minutes all going in the same direction. It may be that the grayling is somewhat alone in the Satyridae and the grass-dependent skippers, in having this penchant for local movement.

Within the strongly migratory whites the brimstone (*Gonepteryx rhamni*) is also prone to local movement. It is often found many kilometres away from its breeding sites and this behaviour in the female is thought to be its way of exploiting new areas. The chief migrants within the 'whites' are the large white and the small white. The green-veined white (*Artogeia napi*) may occur in such numbers that migration may be suspected. The first two species are often seen migrating in company. In fact on very good days for migration, several of the migratory species from the Pieridae and the Nymphalidae may be found together. It is said of the large white that if it were not for the very strong migratory capability of this species throughout Europe, in Britain, at least, it would be a very rare butterfly. This is due to the granulosis virus which decimated the British butterfly population in 1955, thought to have been introduced, incidentally, by migrant large whites. This continual topping-up of populations with migrants is an exceedingly good strategy, well perfected in these butterflies classed as pests. Continual mixing of genes from different regions is good for the species.

The clouded yellows represent a group of migratory pierid butterflies showing much adaptation to continental Europe. They exhibit years of abundance when their numbers flow over into Britain as in 1947, 1955 and 1983. The best year was 1947 when about 36,000 of the clouded yellow (*Colias croceus*) and the pale clouded yellow (*Colias hyale*) were recorded.

RARE MIGRANTS

Rare transatlantic migrants include the monarch and the American painted lady (*Cynthia virginiensis*). The monarch reaches Britain regularly most years but usually in very small numbers. Even fewer of the American painted lady appear. They have been seen along the Portuguese coast and in various places inland in Spain. The largest recorded arrival of monarchs to Britain was 120 in 1981.

The presence of the monarch in Britain is associated with big depressions which sweep across the Atlantic from west to east bringing American birds as well. The butterflies are actually trying to migrate south from North America to their hibernation sites in the south in Mexico. They move southwards in September and may, therefore, have the misfortune to end up 5,500 km away in the west of England or on the west coast of Ireland. Few recorders have seen the monarch in Ireland but in England many sightings have occurred in the West Country. Their milkweed (*Asclepias* spp.) food plants are not generally available for them in the wild in western Europe so there is little chance they will breed. Autumn arrivals have been seen to roost communally in Monterey pines (*Pinus radiata*) in south-west England. Roosting as hibernators is what they are famous for in one locality in Mexico where millions gather each year high up in the forest trees. It is often said that some of the vagrant monarchs could reach Britain by way of the Canaries, where both the monarch and the plain tiger (*Danaus chrysippus*) live. The greater number of insects reaching the south-west of Britain rather than the Continent tends to discount that theory.

The plain tiger does seem to be venturing further afield in Europe from its base in Africa south of the Sahara and from the Canaries where it became established in 1880. It also occurs on the Azores. It is a rare migrant in Morocco and individuals have turned up in southern Italy and Greece. Its course through Spain started in 1980 when it was seen at Alicante in August 1980, at Malaga, Cadiz in 1981 and Murcia in 1982. More recently it has been seen at Narbonne in south-west France in both July and November 1983 and at an air base in Corsica in August 1984.

Lepidopterists in north-west Europe, like Britain, only very rarely come across individuals of the Queen of Spain fritillary (*Issoria lathonia*) which ventures northwards. Around the western part of the Mediterranean it is a fairly common meadow butterfly and a powerful flier. The Bath white (*Pontia daplidice*) is also strongly migratory and common in scabious meadows in southern France but it only very rarely gets as far as Britain. The long-tailed blue (*Lampides boeticus*) is another strongly migratory butterfly which reaches northern France, Belgium and Switzerland and, very occasionally, Britain in the summer. Its relative, the short-tailed blue (*Everes argiades*) is not strongly migratory and it very rarely appears in England. Both of them develop as caterpillars in members of the Leguminosae especially in the kitchen garden.

WHY MIGRATE?

This is the major question asked, but it leads to others. Why do some butterflies spend all of their lives locked up in a tiny meadow, whilst others travel hundreds of kilometres? Why do butterflies fly in regular directions, what guides them, do they use the wind and how far do they fly? These are the sort of questions that are frequently asked, and which lepidopterists are always trying to answer.

It always seems incredible that such a delicate creature as a butterfly can cover hundreds of kilometres across mountains, seas and frontiers

Figure 9.1   The long-tailed blue is a strong migrant in Europe

without apparent difficulty. They seem to be driven on by some innate urge. How many thousands of them kill themselves by setting course westward across the Atlantic, like some of the migratory swarms of African locusts, or are drowned in the North Sea like the ladybirds which form the periodic 'red tides'? Entomologists aboard North Sea oil rigs have recently reported red admirals and small whites, as well as true flies, caddisflies and lacewings on their rigs. Surveys from coastal lighthouses in the past also showed that plenty of insects, not always regular migrants, are found well out to sea.

The main reason for this purposeful cross-country migration is quite clear. It is to get the female away from the place where she grew up as a caterpillar so that she can lay her eggs somewhere else. Overpopulation is a disadvantage since there would not be enough food plants to feed the next generation caterpillars. We have the situation of vast numbers of butterflies developing in certain areas. It would be no use for them to mate and lay their eggs in this restricted area, since their caterpillars would soon devour all the available food plants. It is in the interests of the butterflies to migrate away from this area to discover and exploit new areas and to give rise to a new generation far away from the parental fold. This is the principal reason for migration. Taking them away to a newly colonised area gives them a better chance of survival. Of course this implies it is the female which is the most important sex and has to migrate out of the area. In some cases it is *only* the female which is seen to migrate, but the genetic material locked up in sperms is important too. Baker astutely sums up this important dispersal of genes: 'Every butterfly begins life in a place determined by its mother. Sometime later it dies in a place determined largely by its own behaviour.'

The fact that migratory butterflies appear to fly fairly well defined routes is well known. How they have come to choose this particular path is less clear but the answer may originate in plate tectonics. As continents drift apart so food resources become separated from what once was a neighbouring area in respect of the bird or insect. Over millions of years with the formation of triflingly small increases in the distance between the animal and the food source, so the innate ability to move from one region to another is built up. A migratory movement of tens of thousands of kilometres in a bird is easily matched with the colossal movement of a butterfly or moth. The North American monarch annually does a migration of 3,000 km. Not only does it winter in one region it breeds and feeds in numerous other regions in America and Canada thus dispersing its genes over a large area.

HOW DO THEY MIGRATE?

Butterflies use the position of the sun as a compass for migration and they usually do this between 11.00 and 16.00 hrs. Flying into light winds gives them lift and there are a number of descriptions of migrants doing this. C.B. Williams determined at Harpenden that butterflies like the whites will maintain their direction heading even though the wind may veer from any other direction of the compass. If the wind speed increases too much then flight will be temporarily stopped and the butterfly will rest in vegetation. It is likely that butterflies will be pushed along by the wind, perhaps up to 16 km per hour provided it does not become severe. Large whites have been recorded as flying at over 15 km per hour during sunny weather in the wild. The width of migratory movement is not always possible to determine. In fact the movement of butterflies in one direction may be so spasmodic but regular, say one butterfly crossing a field every two minutes, that the significance may not be grasped for a while. A front of migrating large whites, for example, has been variously recorded at several hundred metres up to 4 km across, involving up to 400 million insects.

Butterflies' energy comes from an entirely different system to that of man. They consume an enormous amount of energy much akin to migratory birds – warblers which take off from Europe may lose half their body weight during their swift flight south to Africa. Birds use up their fat reserves which they have assiduously built up in the weeks prior to migration. Butterflies, on the other hand are born with the energy pack ready for dispersal. They have derived vast stores of yellow body fat, laid down in their abdomen and thorax from food eaten by the caterpillar. The yellow is made up from the carotenoid pigments which are so vital in stalibising important proteins which, being fat soluble, become stored in the fat reserves. It is interesting to note that honey-bees and bumble-bees use up about 10 to 11 mg of sugar per hour when flying.

There is some evidence that butterflies actually feel 'tired' — anthropomorphically speaking. They have been seen coming ashore and alighting immediately on flowers to replenish their sugar reserves. Wild plants like sea lavender (*Limonium* spp. – there are many species), sea aster (*Aster tripolium*) and sea stock (*Matthiola sinuata*) may be covered in migratory species topping up on nectar. This is especially true for the Camargue. There are a few accounts of butterflies landing on water, on boats and taking off again. To take off from water means that it must be very still. Where migratory swarms of butterflies persevere higher and higher up valleys they are likely to succumb to a decrease in temperature, particularly if there is no way through the valley before reaching danger areas. Butterflies have been found embedded in soft snow in the Alps and by a British Everest expedition in the Himalayas and they have been revived with the warmth from the hand.

MIGRATORY ORIGINS?

Where do all these migratory butterflies come from? The mass emergence of butterflies is not witnessed by many people today. One has to root around in the published literature to find any reference to mass emergence of butterflies or of caterpillars swarming over food plants which might suggest a potential source of a migratory swarm.

Climate is a determining factor in the origins of butterfly migrations. The nearer to the centre of a continent the hotter the summer and the colder the winters — a basic geographical fact. It is said that in the Transcaucasia (USSR), Algeria, Tangier, Tripoli, Libya and Syria the large white butterfly may have 5 to 7 generations each year, considerably more than on the Atlantic coast with its variable climate. High rates of reproduction within the USSR compare with those along the southern coast of the Mediterranean. So, eastern Europe and the western USSR are possible sites for the origins of some of our migrations in this species at least.

A consistently warm climate is found in North Africa through which the January 10°C isotherm runs. Here the pleasant Mediterranean climate is much more predictable and gives constant warmth conducive to butterfly metamorphosis. Egg batches laid on one fine day give rise to caterpillars which turn eventually into chrysalises over one or two days, and these give rise to a mass emergence of butterflies on perhaps a single day or spread over two days. The vagaries of storms and anticyclones are not present to disrupt caterpillars in one area compared to another.

The species for which there is evidence that enormous populations of butterflies develop in North Africa include the red admiral and the painted lady. It is interesting to note that the reason often stated for the fact that these two butterflies do not hibernate in Britain is that they cannot survive the adverse effects of the winter climate (i.e. cold and damp). It is abundantly obvious that these two butterflies species are typical Mediterranean butterflies exhibiting great adaptations to the Mediterranean climate. With such clement weather in lowland coastal areas of North Africa it may well be the case that the butterflies, their caterpillars and their chrysalises do not possess sufficient sorbitol in their blood. This carbohydrate is well known as an anti-freeze agent which is present in many butterflies, such as the large white, which are normally subjected to several degrees of frost during the winter. The painted lady occurs throughout the North African countries, from Morocco eastwards to Egypt. In Morocco, where there are several successive generations, the caterpillars are recorded regularly on members of the thistle and mallow families (Compositae and Malvaceae). When the caterpillars become invasive they will also consume watermelon (*Citrullus colocynthis*), vines (*Vitis vinifera*), lucerne (*Medicago sativa*), French or kidney beans (*Phaseolus vulgaris*) and purple viper's bugloss (*Echium lycopsis*). They have also been recorded on cultivated hollyhocks (*Althaea rosea*) and artichokes (*Cynara scolymus*). The arid Sahara zone has a sparse vegetation which supports those butterflies whose caterpillars feed up voraciously during late May and June, giving rise to mass emergence in late June and in July. Many of these individuals are the ones that arrive in north-west Europe from June onwards. Other migratory insects move across the Egyptian deserts where they have been observed. However, the lack of entomologists in what would appear to be the most interesting areas to observe – in Libya, Tunisia and Algeria – results in a paucity of further supportative information concerning this and other species. With regard to the return migration of the painted lady Baker believes that some may find their way down the west coast of Africa.

The Funnelling Effect

Mountains and coastlines frequently exert a funnelling effect on migratory butterflies. Many butterflies, like birds, will follow a coastline in the general direction they are going, rather than cross the sea. Thus southerly moving insects and birds in south-east England are projected across the water from points such as Dungeness in Kent — which is noted as a region of international importance because of this particular phenomenon. Others include Spurn Head (East Riding of Yorkshire), Portland Bill (Dorset) and Cap de la Hage (Manche, northern France). In the case of Dungeness this does not provide the shortest sea crossing (40 km instead of 32 km), a point that the insects are not likely to appreciate.

In north-west Europe the rapid onset of inhospitable autumns puts paid to any significant, if detectable, return migration. In southern Europe it is a different matter. The weather is much better, less damp and the glorious sunshine and higher temperatures often extend into October and prolong the life of butterflies. A southerly migration is more pronounced, particularly for those butterflies leaving France. Butterflies following the Mediterranean coast can filter into Spain via the coastal plain near Perpignan or Biarritz on the Atlantic coast. Here it is much more mountainous and butterflies may well be pushed into Portugal or up into the Basque mountains. For butterflies and other insects migrating south well inland in France it just so happens that the natural alignment of the mountain ridges funnels them into certain valleys. Here their numbers are concentrated as they pour over passes. The Pyrénées has always been a place of pilgrimage for entomologists interested in this phenomenon and locations like the Cols of Gavarnie, Puymorens, Portalet, Quillane, the Ports of Venasques and the Portachuelo Pass have yielded spectacular movements of insects in the past. Many of these sites have 'V' shaped passes through which insects are funnelled.

The mass movement of insects in the Pyrénées can be quite astounding. The most prolific insects are hoverflies recorded at up to 100,000 per hour, followed by dragonflies at 1,000 an hour. Birds, beetles and moths such as the day-flier and hibernator, the humming-bird hawk-moth (*Macroglossum stellatarum*) funnel through alongside regular migrants such as red admirals and Bath whites. Figures for butterflies are not available, but occasional sightings of swallowtails, fritillaries and blues have been recorded. Anytime between mid-September and mid-October seems to be the period during which a migratory stream may be encountered. There are many areas through which the butterflies could wander and one cannot be precise about the day and place. The weather conditions have to be right with a lack of cloud enveloping the mountains, a feature of the Pyrénées not always experienced during the high summer. A fine sunny day with little or no wind is ideal. Most migration of butterflies is thought to occur fairly close to the ground, but there is a unique case of a glider pilot in northern Germany who encountered migrating large whites at an altitude of 1,200 to 1,700 m.

10 Conservation

'Who are you, aged man?' I said.
'And how is it you live?'
And his answer trickled through my head·
Like water through a sieve.

He said 'I look for butterflies
That sleep among the wheat:
I make them into mutton-pies,
And sell them on the street.'

Lewis Carroll (1832–98) *Through the Looking Glass*

INTRODUCTION

No other animal is more typical of a healthy environment, nor more susceptible to change, than a butterfly. They monitor the well-being of a habitat just as lichens make excellent pollution-monitors. People expect butterflies in wild places; places where nature is brimming over with living things. Butterflies epitomise the natural environment and are sadly missed when things go wrong.

Compared with their European neighbours Britain's butterflies are more severely threatened since Britain has the highest population – some 56 million people in a relatively small island. As we shall see butterflies thrive in areas with low human frequentation and are now found in greater numbers in restricted areas than in comparable-sized areas where people have free access.

Conservationists use a variety of different terms to describe the well-being of plants and animals. What then, do terms like vulnerable, threatened and endangered really mean? A species is either 'extant' (i.e. still living) or 'extinct' (meaning that the individuals have died out). Technically, to be extinct a living thing must not be found within 50 years of its being extant. Populations move from being perfectly healthy to extinct via the labels of 'rare', 'vulnerable' and 'endangered'.

'Rare' species have very localised populations which are at risk. They are likely to become vulnerable or endangered if the circumstances change for the worse. Examples of rare species in Europe include the greenish black tip (*Elphinstonia charlonia*), Ottoman's brassy ringlet (*Erebia ottomana*), the Sardinian meadow brown (*Maniola nurag*) and the pigmy skipper (*Gegenes pumilio*). A 'vulnerable' species is one whose population is decreasing and which is likely to become endangered if the decline continues. In Europe 50 species are classified as vulnerable and many are mentioned in this book; four which are not previously mentioned are the peak white (*Pontia chloridice*), Freyer's purple emperor (*Apatura metis*), Lorkovic's brassy ringlet (*Erebia calcaria* and the false eros blue (*Polyommatus eroides*). 'Endangered' species are those which are in danger of extinction and whose populations are dangerously low. Any slight change in their environment is likely to kill them off. Amongst others mentioned in this book are the Dalmatian ringlet (*Erebia phegea*), bog fritillary (*Proclossiana eunomia*), large copper (*Lycaena dispar*) and the dusky large blue (*Maculinea nausithous*). A 'threatened' population may have reached any of these three stages and those species for which information is lacking are described as being 'indeterminate'. Comparison of distribution maps may also indicate 'declining' populations and these are those whose populations have decreased by 10 per cent since 1960.

The most up to date review of the conservation of European butterflies, published in 1984, is by Jeremy Thomas in *The Biology of the Butterflies* to which readers are referred. Readers are also directed to the excellent work of Heath, Pollard and Thomas, *Atlas of Butterflies in Britain and Ireland* (1985) which gives so many details on the ecology and conservation of butterflies.

The aim of this chapter, then, is to draw attention to the horrendous decline in Europe's butterflies through habitat loss, to examine the factors detrimentally affecting butterflies and to discuss some of the conservation strategies to protect butterflies. One could write a separate book solely on the effect of habitat loss on butterfly ecology, but it has seemed more reasonable here to focus attention on the more positive aspects of butterfly conservation.

The Nature Conservancy Council are so right when they say '... just 40 years ago, not only was it possible to walk miles amongst a myriad butterflies but the scene could almost be taken for granted. Today, such a sight, even on a small piece of ground, is a rare moment worthy of comment'.

HABITAT LOSS

In Europe the greatest threat to butterflies has been habitat loss. The effects of pollution, collecting and specific butterfly diseases pale in comparison. Habitat loss is the symptom of post-war agriculture. Large fields were created at the expense of the hedgerows. In Britain the peak of hedgerow removal was during 1962–6 when, in eastern England, 5,600 km per year were being grubbed out. Woods became islands in a sea of agricultural land. Copses and rough marginal land disappeared – as a chapter title from Marion Shoard's forthright book *The Theft of the Countryside* (1980) puts it so aptly, 'subsidies for destruction' were handed out by the government (they still are) for conversion of marginal land into land capable of growing a crop. Here is not the place to discuss the effects of the European Economic Commission (EEC) policy on agricultural practices. Suffice it to say that a calamitous amount of land (comprising many habitats) has been laid waste to feed people in Europe; and, that no political party, of whatever persuasion, is ever likely to protect wildlife at the expense of feeding its people. Compromises between naturalists and politicians are the answer.

Marginal land is a general term which implies rough pastures often on soils of low fertility. It could also be a synonym for a good butterfly habitat. Examples of marginal land include heathland, steep downland with scrub and wetlands. Each of these habitats offers different species of butterflies an opportunity to breed. Draining of the land is a good and proper practice of farmers which, unlike the other farming practices detrimental to the butterflies, has been going on for millennia. (The author can speak from both sides, as a farmer's son and as a conservationist.)

Habitat loss is caused by a number of agricultural practices, of which ploughing of ancient pastures, hedge-removal, woodland removal and drainage play their part. It is ironic that the decline in upkeep of some habitats, for instance coppice management may be detrimental to one species – the pearl-bordered fritillary (*Clossiana euphrosyne*) because of disappearing violet food plants – and beneficial to another – white admiral (*Ladoga camilla*) – because of increase in honeysuckle.

Quantitative evidence implicating agricultural practices in the downfall of butterflies is very hard to find. Unlike dead mammals or birds, like otters or ospreys, dead butterflies do not persist long enough to be discovered and taken in for investigation. It is thought by some that the effects of agrichemicals (the combined attack from insecticides, herbicides, fungicides and acaracides) in the countryside is not that serious. In fact in some other over-polluted habitats, such as along motorways, insects (particularly moths) seem to thrive. However, there is contradictory evidence that some butterflies have reproductive problems in the same situation.

John Heath believes that 4 per cent of the 362 European species of butterfly face extinction today and a further 14 per cent are 'vulnerable'. Denmark has lost one species, and East Germany and Finland have lost others. In Belgium 13 of the original 118 species have now become extinct. Of the 60 species recorded in Holland up to 1981, 9 are now extinct, 11 were not seen in 1981, 28 are rare and 13 locally abundant. Only a dozen of Holland's butterfly species are now regarded as common. The future of Europe's butterflies looks very grim.

One exception appears to be in Italy where, according to Emilio Balletto and his colleagues, 'one can practically state that no Italian species of butterfly has apparently become extinct in the last two centuries'. Balletto has recorded 234 species in Italy and its major islands. The only exception is Ripart's anomalous blue (*Agrodiaetus ripartii*), which may well have become extinct due to natural afforestation. Some Italian butterflies, like the false ringlet (*Coenonympha oedippus*) and the large chequered skipper (*Heteropterus morpheus*) may succumb in the future to intensive agriculture in the Po valley. Development of coastal habitats for tourism, so common elsewhere around the Mediterranean and Atlantic coasts, denies butterflies this particular habitat.

Indirectly the rabbit has been associated with the decline of several butterfly species in Britain; the large blue butterfly was declared extinct in 1979, as an indirect result of the lack of rabbits. Rabbits are alien to Britain and were introduced by the Normans and kept in warrens. It was only in the eighteenth century that they escaped and became as common as we know them today. The introduction of the myxomatosis virus killed off large populations of rabbits throughout much of Europe. The effect on the well-nibbled grasslands was to encourage the growth of tall coarser grasses. Butterfly food plants became crowded out and gravid females could not find their food plants on which to oviposit. This was the sad story of the demise of the large blue from its last stronghold in Cornwall. Rabbits have survived this onslaught of myxomatosis and have evolved a sort of 'scrub rabbit' which stayed above ground in times of danger. Those that bolted down a hole were more likely to be bitten by fleas which transmit the myxomatosis virus. Fortunately for some butterflies, rabbits resistant to myxomatosis are still efficient grazers and keep many areas down to a short grassland sward sufficient for caterpillar food plants to thrive.

The large blue butterfly in England was the most well known victim to succumb to habitat change through the loss of rabbits from myxomatosis, though it still flies on many a hillside on the Continent where myxomatosis is rife. It has been suggested that populations of six other species of butterfly — mostly blues — the small blue (*Cupido minimus*), the common blue (*Polyommatus icarus*) the chalkhill blue (*Lysandra coridon*), the silver-spotted skipper (*Hesperia comma*), the high brown fritillary (*Argynnis adippe*) and from 70 to 80 per cent of British colonies of the adonis blue (*Lysandra bellargus*) have also been lost through the development of long grass indirectly caused by myxomatosis. In managing grassland habitats for the chequered skipper (*Carterocephalus palaemon*) it is thought that the return of the rabbit to its large pre-myxomatosis levels might contribute to the controlled grazing necessary.

COLLECTING

As an ardent non-collector I must say that the traditional collecting of butterflies was as innocent as collecting flowers. In wild unspoilt meadows it is quite natural for children to pick handfuls of flowers and chase butterflies. Both flowers and butterflies were always very common. They symbolise everything that's good about habitats. It almost seems that true country people show an innate consciousness for collecting. Their depredations make very little difference to the local populations of both wild flowers or butterflies. The problem is a question of degree.

With the countryside under increasing pressure from man, butterfly-human interactions increase much to the detriment of the insects. Present day lepidopterists have been very slow to shrug off the Victorian passion to collect everything that moves, is colourful and is a little different. The current response in justifying collecting might be 'I only take a couple of examples', instead of a long series. Butterflies have had such a hammering through habitat loss that any form of collecting is likely to prejudice their chances of survival. Lepidopterists are now only just past the stage that ornithologists were at during the last century when egg-collecting was in vogue. Birding is the major preoccupation of naturalists and their enthusiasm prospers now without collecting eggs. In answer to the question: 'Why conserve butterflies?' the Nature Conservancy Council are keen to say that 'they are attractive and give us pleasure in the countryside and garden'. That is plenty of justification to leave them alone.

Figure 10.1   Thyme plants are typical of chalky areas and often grow on ant hills

The apollo (*Parnassius apollo*) is in a special category of its own since some over-zealous lepidopterists still seek to collect it in all of its last mountain strongholds. Although it is offered some protection in Appendix II of the *Convention on International Trade in Endangered Species of Wild Fauna and Flora* (C.I.T.E.S.) there are still ruthless collectors who hunt it in the Pyrénées, Massif Central, Alps, the Pieniny mountains of Poland and the Scandinavian mountains. Elsewhere in Europe other butterflies are under threat from collectors: the Spanish festoon (*Zerynthia rumina*) in the Alpes-Maritimes, Basse-Alpes and in Spain; the monarch (*Danaus plexippus*) in the Canaries; the Corsican swallowtail (*Papilio hospiton*) both on Corsica and Sardinia; Ratzer's ringlet (*Erebia christi*) in Switzerland and Italy; and the Gavarnie blue (*Agriades pyrenaicus*) in France. In Britain there is a useful *Code for Insect Collecting* prepared by the Joint Committee for the Conservation of British Insects (J.C.C.B.I.). (Copies are obtainable from the Royal Entomological Society, 41, Queen's Gate, London, SW7 5HU.) Some local or national protection in the form of collecting restrictions is provided in Austria, Czechoslovakia, Finland, France, Switzerland and West Germany. However, the compilers of the I.U.C.N. *Invertebrate Red Data Book* feel, quite correctly, that habitat loss is the major threat to apollos today. Too many mountains in Europe become planted up with undistinguished conifers.

Emilio Balletto in Italy describes the Sicilian subspecies of the apollo (*P.a. siciliae*) and the Corsican swallowtail as 'overcollected panoramic (*sic*) species'. Unfortunately these are still persistently pursued and he argues for the establishment of nature reserves and legislation to help. He also maintains that the Grecian anomalous blue (*Agrodiaetus aroaniensis* subspecies *humedasae* is at risk from collecting in North Italy. In Spain it is argued that a special nature reserve for apollos should be set up in the Pyrénées which would protect other forms of wildlife as well.

Other species which have always been susceptible to collecting because of their fine colours or curious life style, are the purple emperor (*Apatura iris*) — over 100 were once collected from an Essex wood in a fortnight — and of course the large blue (*Maculinea arion*); in 1939 a collection was found to have 770 specimens! Large blues were obviously much commoner towards the end of the last century and a collector could net 1,000 specimens in a season.

In England, the heath fritillary (*Mellicta athalia*) has suffered its share of collecting. At the end of the last century 'professional exchangers and dealers' systematically wiped out various colonies in Kent by 1880. Today its last major stand in Britain is in the region of Canterbury and its habitats managed by various nature conservation bodies. It is 'protected' from collecting by the Wildlife and Countryside Act (1981) — meaning that it is an offence to collect any stage or destroy the habitat. Fines and/or imprisonment are penalties for not upholding the law but so far it has not been tested.

It is easy to blame wanton collecting for the decline of various species, but in some species they become rare or extinct due to reasons beyond the control of man. The chequered skipper became extinct in England, from its 54 East Midland colonies, probably due to habitat change. The black-veined white (*Aporia crataegi*) became extinct in England probably due to a decrease in the viability of its last remaining stock or from orchard spraying. There is some controversy about the reason for the demise of the large copper; it was supposedly extinct, due to collecting, by 1850, but specimens have since been located which were collected from the Fens during the period 1880–92, whilst in the Norfolk Broads specimens collected up to 1918 have now been found. Attempts to introduce the large copper on Wheatfen Broad in 1949 were unsuccessful due to winter flooding.

Fortunately some butterflies escape the depredations of collectors simply because of their way of life or choice of habitat, like the black hairstreak (*Strymonidia pruni*) which spends much of its time on the canopy of oak woods or the bog fritillary (*Boloria aquilonaria*) which flies over Danish peat bogs, previously excavated in the Second World War and which are now impossible to walk on. Some butterfly species find themselves within military land and are not subject to the usual rigours of the agricultural environment. They prosper and represent a fine reservoir of wildlife as a contingency for the future.

WHAT CAN BE DONE?
Understanding Butterfly Ecology from Mapping Schemes

There are two useful ways of assessing the welfare of butterflies: by using a national mapping system and by locally monitoring the butterflies. Both systems have been pioneered in the United Kingdom and are now in use in Europe and the United States. The national mapping system was originated by John Heath at the Institute of Terrestrial Ecology's Biological Records Centre in Cambridgeshire in the 1960s and is based on the country divided up into 10 × 10 sq km 'tetrads'. The idea was copied from the botanists. Recorders are encouraged to send in local data which is put onto the maps in the form of a filled-in dot indicating recent presence. In England sufficient information has now been incorporated into the maps to show a meaningful distribution, rather than where keen lepidopterists lived or went on holiday (unfortunately, due to a lack of recorders, this is sometimes the case in Scotland and Eire).

Several European countries operate a national mapping system but nowhere else in Europe is the interest so high as in Britain and Ireland where there are now nearly 2,000 recorders. (This compares to Holland with 200; theirs was established in 1980, and is based upon tetrads of 5 × 5 sq km.) The fruits of 20 years work of collecting data on the United Kingdom butterflies is now shown in a series of maps in the most valuable *Atlas of Butterflies in Britain and Ireland* — a definitive statement of the well-being of the 55 resident species. There are also a few local mapping systems in Britain and Ireland undertaken by local museums and county trusts for nature conservation using 1 sq km tetrads.

The national mapping system admirably shows the current distribution of butterflies but it gives little indication of local fluctuations in butterfly numbers. Such information is vital in the conservation of butterflies. Here the butterfly monitoring scheme devised by Ernest Pollard of Monks Wood comes into its own. This system was established in 1976 and relies upon naturalists walking a defined path every week during the butterfly season and recording all the butterflies seen. So far over 80 volunteer recorders work in the field reporting back information from all over Britain on the welfare of their local butterflies. The advantages are clear. Local fluctuations can be detected as soon as the data is compared with other regional information. If a habitat is being destroyed or is changing to a different type, some management action could be instigated to save a particular species. The British Butterfly Conservation Society also makes regional surveys of butterfly species but they are particularly interested in the threatened species.

Legislation and Conservation

Some degree of legislative control of butterflies is now afforded by the governments of a few European countries. It represents a start, but it falls short of what many people would like to see. Like much legislation it becomes out of date from the moment of publication and extinctions of listed butterflies may occur even before publication date. Short lists of critical species recommended for inclusion in any legislative document may themselves be shortened, so that many other deserving species do not become officially incorporated. Anomalies therefore occur.

It is customary for these restrictive laws to forbid the taking of all life stages of the butterfly concerned, or to travel with them, sell them or purchase them. Possession of every single specimen, say a box of 20 caterpillars, may be regarded as 20 offences. Destruction or disturbing the habitat is also covered by some countries. In effect, the laws which govern collecting of butterflies are incredibly difficult to police, for example the novice or casual (child) collector may not know sufficient to identify the difference between a common species and a protected one.

Despite these shortcomings, it is imperative to have legislative control of collecting. In the field of ornithology plenty of prosecutions relate to egg-collecting each year in Britain, simply because law enforcement officers of a voluntary conservation body (the Royal Society for the Protection of Birds) keep up a high level of enquiry and detection. At present, with most of the European butterflies unprotected from collecting, it is still legal to amass series of butterflies and to bring them through under the eyes of customs officials who are helpless to do anything. There are still some lepidopterists today who specifically set out to collect long series of butterflies from some of the vulnerable habitats in Europe (for instance in the mountains of the Pyrénées and Alps) despite many efforts to protect

Table 10.1 Countries in which the following butterflies and their subspecies have some sort of legislative protection. See John Heath's *Threatened Rhopalocera in Europe* and the laws pertinent to each country for full details

Butterfly species

Common English name	Latin name	AUSTRIA	CZECHOSLOVAKIA	FINLAND	FRANCE	GERMANY (DDR)	LUXEMBOURG	NETHERLANDS	POLAND	SWEDEN	SWITZERLAND	UNITED KINGDOM	USSR, LITHUANIA SSR
Hesperiidae													
chequered skipper	*Carterocephalus palaemon*											✓	
Papilionidae													
swallowtail	*Papilio machaon*	✓	✓								✓	✓	
Corsican swallowtail	*Papilio hospiton*	✓	✓		✓	✓					✓		
scarce swallowtail	*Iphiclides podalirius*	✓	✓										
southern festoon	*Zerynthia polyxena*	✓	✓	✓	✓	✓	✓				✓		
Spanish festoon	*Zerynthia rumina* form *honorati*				✓								
apollo	*Parnassius apollo*								✓				✓
	subspecies *arvernensis*				✓								
	subspecies *francisci*				✓								
	subspecies *meridionalis*				✓								
small apollo	*Parnassius phoebus*												
clouded apollo	*Parnassius mnemosyne*		✓	✓		✓			✓		✓		
Pieridae													
mountain small white	*Pieris ergane*				✓								
moorland clouded yellow	*Colias palaeno* female only				✓								

Nymphalidae

purple emperor	Apatura iris
lesser purple emperor	Apatura ilia
poplar admiral	Ladoga populi
Camberwell beauty	Nymphalis antiopa
large tortoiseshell	Nymphalis polychloros
red admiral	Vanessa atalanta
peacock	Inachis io
bog fritillary	Proclossiana eunomia
cranberry fritillary	Boloria aquilonaris
Frigga's fritillary	Clossiana frigga
heath fritillary	Mellicta athalia
Spanish fritillary	Euphdryas desfontainii

Satyridae

large heath	Coenonympha tullia
false ringlet	Coenonympha eodippus female only
Baltic grayling	Oeneis jutta
wall brown	Lasiommata megera
woodland brown	Lopinga achine

Lycaenidae

violet copper	Lycaena helle
large copper	Lycaena dispar (female only — France only)
scarce large blue	Maculinea telejus subspecies burdigalensis female only
large blue	Maculinea arion
Alcon blue	Maculinea alcon female only
Adonis blue	Lysandra bellargus form coelestis

the butterfly's fragile refuges. National Parks exist for the recreation of people as well as the conservation of the wildlife. It must be remembered that it is often forbidden to collect any form of wildlife on any of the thousands of nature reserves now designated throughout Europe.

The British Parliament published The Wildlife and Countryside Act (1981) which afforded protection for four species of butterfly (Table 10.1). In 1983 the French list (which covers other non-European countries of the Republic of France) gave protection to several species, and subspecies in France and its Mediterranean islands. In Belgium bans on collecting, trading of living or dead specimens and laws giving special protection for habitats are designed to conserve their vulnerable species.

When an endangered species exists as only a few individuals, emotions are aroused as to the best method of conserving it. Legislation may be drawn up, guards may be stationed around the habitat and everyone becomes most concerned. The species itself may receive enormous media coverage and be featured on the front pages of national papers. But legislation at this stage is far too late. The plant or animal species may not be numerous enough to maintain a viable population. Genetic disorders may creep in due to inbreeding. The answer, in retrospect, is to pass legislation pertinent to an earlier stage in the well-being of that now endangered species. Protection of habitats is vital for protecting common species today which may become the endangered species of tomorrow.

The respect with which the last genetic stock of an endangered species is treated varies with the individual philosophy of nature conservation. Do you leave the species alone, or relieve it of some genetic material and rear it up in a 'better' environment? Although there are regulations controlling the trade in eggs of rare species it is interesting to note that in Spain, one of the conservation measures to protect, in this case, a rare moth (*Graellsia isabellae*), is to offer the eggs to interested people for an increase in numbers of that species. In the botanical world, dividing tubers of rare orchids has been successful – where in Kent the tubers of the monkey orchid (*Orchis morio*) have been legally dug up and planted on similar habitats with great success. Others would argue that it is sacrilege to play around with a vulnerable population. It *is* worth taking the risk.

Positive conservation work to save butterflies and their habitats is going on in several European countries. This is manifest in three ways: urgently investigating the ecology of the butterfly (often at an ineffective late stage); tending the habitat; and making introductions or re-introductions.

Dwindling populations of the apollo butterflies are receiving much attention in southern Finland and south-west Germany (*Parnassius apollo* and *P.a. marcianus*) respectively. Curiously the German butterfly population in the Black Forest is still maintaining its numbers on a steep railway embankment, despite heavy atmospheric pollution. The German scientists tackled the problem of how to increase numbers in both countries by relieving gravid females of the eggs in the wild and trying to rear them on in the laboratory. They were not too successful since the *Sedum* food plant was not easy to grow in quantity. The butterfly habitats were however boosted with the re-introduction of half-grown caterpillars to fend for themselves. It was hoped that caterpillars might also be released in habitats formerly occupied by the butterflies. No positive steps to protect the apollo or clouded apollo (*Parnassius mnemosyne*) on Mt Aigoual in the Parc National des Cévennes is currently in operation.

Introductions

Numerous attempts at introduction and re-introduction of butterflies have been made throughout Europe. Many have gone unrecorded since amateur lepidopterists release excess breeding stock or livestock collected on travels. Few introductions have been carefully monitored and set up after extensive habitat management.

The terms 'introduction' and 're-introduction' are frequently misused and need definition. Re-introduction (or re-establishment), as the word suggests, means to liberate the insect into a habitat where it once lived. An introduction is where an insect is liberated in any other area.

The whole question of whether it is right to introduce or re-introduce an insect is a very controversial subject. It is in everyone's interests to be aware of what introductions are taking place; thus any intended introduction should be carefully discussed with local naturalists' groups. In any case, many regional conservation organisations (especially in England) exercise a code of conduct regarding introductions, whether plant or animal drawn up by the J.C.C.B.I.

It is quite understandable to see how lepidopterists in the past felt stimulated to release butterflies into the wild. By far the commonest motivation has come from seeing a population of a rare butterfly dwindle. The need to replace or supplement a dying colony with new stock has been great. There are few examples of trying to establish a butterfly quite alien to the country from another country. The celebrated example in England is that of the map butterfly (*Araschnia levana*) which was liberated in the Forest of Dean (Gwent) in about 1912 and another population near Symond's Yat (Herefordshire and Worcestershire). The colonies prospered for several years but were systematically killed off by a collector hostile to such an alien introduction.

One of the main reasons for vetting introductions is to eliminate indiscriminate movement of species from one place to another. Even the introductions of very common species should be reported to local naturalists' organisations so that the information can filter back to the regional and national bodies which monitor butterfly distribution. Antagonists would argue that hybridisation between, say, two closely related subspecies, would upset the genetics and the external features (phenotype) of the original species.

When a species becomes close to extinction there is very little that can be done to save it. You could argue that it is not worth even trying to re-introduce a closely related subspecies since you can be very sure that it will not have the exact physiological adaptations for the particular habitat. It may come from a different country, a different latitude and a slightly different habitat, so it is not 'programmed' (evolved) to be adjusted to the vagaries of the new habitat to which it has been introduced. Furthermore it may also cause genetic upsets.

To be objective there are few introductions and re-introductions which have been successful without considerable help from man. Those that have survived several years have done so because the habitat has been managed or their life stages have been individually pampered. Left on their own they do not naturally prosper. Having highlighted an area of futility in butterfly introductions I must say that I am in favour of replacing endangered species with similar examples from wherever you can get them, from other countries, or general breeding stock. But not everyone agrees with this. Butterflies are such innocuous and pretty insects, we all deserve to have them in our gardens, cities and in the countryside. Speaking of the map butterfly Professor E.B. Ford said: 'I should not object to a further attempt being made to naturalize it in this country'.

Displeasure at the folly of introducing the British race of the brimstone (*Gonepteryx rhamni*) into Tipperary (Eire) was expressed when a hybrid population of English and Irish butterflies eventually resulted. But the greatest mix up of genes debate centred around the introductions of large coppers (*Lycaena dispar*) into Tipperary earlier this century. The story needs some unravelling since it involves butterflies from Germany, Holland, England and Eire.

There were three subspecies involved; *L.d. dispar* from England, *L.d. batavus* from Holland and *L.d. rutilus* from Germany. Captain W.B. Purefoy prepared a snipe bog habitat in Tipperary with appropriate food plants (great water dock, *Rumex hydrolapathum*) and in 1913 introduced 120 larvae of *rutilus* collected in the marshes north of Berlin. The following year he released about 400 adults bred from his German stock. The habitat must have been very suitable for the butterflies thrived until 1936. Then some stock of Dutch origin (*batavus*), which had been introduced to Woodwalton Fen (Cambridgeshire), was taken from there and further introduced to the Irish locality. Unfortunately the bog began

Figure 10.2   Large water dock can be over a metre high and grow in very damp conditions

to terrestrialise (dry up) and the butterflies eventually died out in 1955. However, they left a legacy of hybrid sotck, of *dispar* males × *rutilus* females and *rutilus* males × *dispar* females, collected specimens of which now resides in the Tring Collection at the British Museum (Natural History).

Back in East Anglia steps were well on the way to conserve a locality especially for butterflies. The Hon Charles Rothschild (Miriam Rothschild's father) bought Woodwalton Fen in 1910 and gave it to the Society for the Protection of Nature Conservation (now the Royal Society for Nature Conservation). The scrub-encroached wetland habitat was thinned and planted with large water dock especially for re-introductions of the large copper. The Irish *rutilus* stock was used to stock the Woodbastwick Marshes in the Bure Valley and 400 pupae were brought over. The butterflies thrived for two years but died out due to habitat mismanagement. The 'Copper Field' was prepared in 1926 with masses of large water dock ready for imported *rutilus* from North Friesland (Holland) in 1927. By the following summer over 1,000 butterflies were on the wing despite the chrysalises being submerged during the previous winter. In 1953 Woodwalton Fen became a National Nature Reserve and today this re-introduced colony still thrives after 50 years of management. In 1931 *batavus* was also re-introduced successfully into the Wicken Sedge Fen (Cambridgeshire) but has now died out.

Meticulous attention must be given to butterfly habitats when any introduction and re-introduction is being undertaken and it is surprising how often man-managed habitats are suitable. The large copper still survives in abandoned peat cuttings in Holland and in Italy it has flourished in rice fields. However in both countries the species is declining due to habitat loss (both natural regeneration and drainage) and possibly agricultural chemicals, particularly herbicides eliminated the food plant. In northern France the butterfly has survived in the départements of Meuse and Meurthe-et-Moselle, but in Belgium has declined in the wet meadows in the Semois valley (the Semois drains off the Ardennes mountains and flows into the River Meuse) since 1940. Much earlier the subspecies, *L.d. gronieri* became extinct in the Marais de Saint Quentin (Aisne) in 1908.

Big upsets in the ecology of butterfly habitats may cause extinction in some species. It is therefore imperative to be wary of variable weather conditions. The large copper may be able to survive submersion by flooding, but the English subspecies of swallowtail (*Papilio machaon*) cannot seem to survive drought. On the Continent it positively thrives in the drought conditions which regularly afflict the southern part of France and which also stimulates its other food plants. A great deal of trouble was exercised at the Wicken Sedge Fen to re-introduce the swallowtail in 1975 following its extinction there in 1952. Milk parsley (*Peucedanum palustre*) (some 3,500 specimens) were encouraged to grow very tall, just as the gravid females prefer, and 228 adults were liberated. The experiment had every sign of success with an estimated 20,000 eggs laid and 2,000 caterpillars forming chrysalises. Unfortunately the severe drought of 1976 curtailed plant growth which had a knock-on effect on the butterflies. They are now extinct at Wicken, but fortunately survive in isolated pockets in the Norfolk Broads.

The heath fritillary has been the subject of introductions and re-introductions for over 50 years in England, yet despite this it is now a threatened and protected species. Loss of habitat through neglecting coppice woodland management is the main factor. The butterfly has been introduced, or suspected to have been introduced, in various Essex woods in 1925 and 1935, re-introduced into Abbots Wood (Huntingdonshire) in about 1935 and also into Aldershot (Hampshire) and Woolmer Forest (Hampshire). The Hockley (Essex) introduction is thought to have survived for 40 years. Another fritillary, the Glanville (*Melitaea cinxia*) in Britain confined to the southern coast line of the Isle of Wight, has also had a chequered history of introductions, also into Woolmer Forest, the Wirral Peninsula (Cheshire) in 1945 and into the New Forest (Hampshire). Other nymphalids introduced by man include the silver-washed fritillary (*Argynnis paphia*) re-introduced at Ipswich (Suffolk) in 1945, and the high brown (possibly assisted by car) in 1941 to the Argyll island of Islay from the mainland. Europe has been instrumental in establishing butterflies and other insects into other continents, for instance the red admiral (*Vanessa atalanta*) and the small white (*Pieris rapae*) into New Zealand and the large white (*Pieris brassicae*) into South America.

The blues and hairstreaks have been the subject of various introductions. The pretty adonis blue died out at one of its favourite localities, Old Winchester Hill (Hampshire) in the late 1950s through development of long grass following myxomatosis. It was re-introduced in the 1970s (60 butterflies) and within three generations had increased to a staggering 5,000 individuals. In Wales 90 specimens of the silver-studded blue (*Plebejus argus*) were liberated in 1942 in the Dulas valley near Rhyd-y-Foel, and, following genetic problems, became abundant in 1953–9. Meticulous study of the variation in the orange lunules on the female hind wing upperside, and the extent of violet-blue colour on the upper female fore wing, has been carried out by Roger Dennis to establish changes in populations in Gwynedd, Clwyd and Dumfries and Galloway. Another Lycaenid butterfly, the black hairstreak (*Strymonidia pruni*), re-introduced into Abbots Wood (east Sussex) and Monk's Wood (Cambridgeshire), has prospered well.

The black-veined white has been the subject of several re-introductions following its extinction in Britain in east Kent in about 1925. The well known lepidopterist L. Hugh Newman recalls that Continental stock was re-introduced near Sandwich (Kent) between 1930–40. In 1948 and 1949 an experiment was made at re-introducing the butterflies in Winston Churchill's garden, at Chartwell, Westerham (Kent) but this suffered from bird predation. The butterfly was apparently living in east Kent in 1964. In the mid-1970s hundreds of Continental butterflies were released at Holmwood Common (Surrey) but they did not survive. The latest attempts to re-introduce the black-veined white from the Continent look very promising. Eggs from a Spanish locality were brought to Fife, north of Edinburgh, in 1974 and produced 300 butterflies in the two following years. It was supplemented with other butterflies from the Swiss/Italian border in 1978.

Conservation on Military Land

Nothing is quite like a prohibited zone for conserving butterflies. Man-the-picker-trampler-and-collector is denied access and wildlife flourishes. Surprisingly you might think that an area swarming with military men and machines might be quite a hostile environment for butterflies. The opposite is true. Butterflies are now overflowing on the ranges and the military are actually very pleased about it.

Throughout Europe, military enclosures attract much wildlife, not only butterflies but wild plants, birds, mammals and reptiles enjoy the relatively undisturbed wastelands. In fact birding 'twitchers' frequently get too close to the sensitive air base of Istres on the eastern edge of the Camargue. In Norway the Arctic woodland ringlet (*Erebia medusa polaris*) thrives around the demolished German forts still protected from grazing animals by barbed wire. Here the caterpillar food plant millet grass (*Milium effusum*) grows well and the butterflies are numerous.

In Britain the wildlife on military sites is continually monitored in a highly efficient exercise. Each area has a contingent of dedicated amateur naturalists amongst the military personnel who prepare notes on most forms of wildlife. Local professional and amateur naturalists act in a supporting role and the annual collated results are published in the journal *Sanctuary*. The Ministry of Defence (MOD) acknowledge that they are guardians of a substantial part of our wildlife heritage and employ a conservation officer to co-ordinate all the information. Many of the MOD sites are recognised by the government's watchdog committee on conservation, the Nature Conservancy Council. Their designation of Sites of Special Scientific Interest (S.S.S.I.) given to selected sites is meant to offer some sort of legislative control. Unfortunately, it doesn't always.

A great deal of military land comprises residential quarters, and marginal land such as moors, scrub and woodland — ample refuges for wildlife. Even in training areas which receive as many as 80,000 troops a year wildlife thrives. Many training grounds are on heathlands rich in typical heathland flora and fauna. In Britain, heathlands are one of the most endangered habitats and have been disappearing rapidly since the turn of the century. Enclosing vast areas and restricting access from the public serves to conserve valuable wildlife habitats from the detrimental effects of man. Some of these habitats were originally enclosed from virgin countryside (like many of the churchyards) and the flora and fauna has therefore remained intact — a relic in a sea of otherwise 'improved' agricultural land. Insects have consequently benefited and have definitely prospered in some areas.

There are now more butterfly species living successfully inside the perimeter of MOD sites in England, than in equivalent sized areas of the ordinary countryside. All the nasty developments and practices of man have eliminated many butterflies from much of the unenclosed countryside. Few of these have ventured onto MOD land. The problems caused by military manoeuvres pales into insignificance in relation to gross habitat loss the other side of the fence.

There are now eleven MOD sites which have more than 30 species of butterfly living there – nearly half the possible number on the British list – (Table 10.2). Purple emperors even fly at Greenham Common (Berkshire) as well as marsh fritillaries (*Euphydras aurinia*); the latter noted also at Imber in Wiltshire where it has had a population explosion over the last decade thanks to military protection. On the Lulworth ranges the dark green fritillary (*Argynnis aglaja*) flies. Ditton Park (Berkshire) still sports 18 species of butterfly, including the white admiral (*Ladoga camilla*) despite it being in the flight path of Heathrow jets which pour out kerosene

Table 10.2 Top MOD butterfly sites
With 30 or more butterfly species

Aldermaston, Berkshire
Bordon-Longmoor, Hampshire
Bramley, Hampshire
Chatham, Kent
Farnborough, Hampshire
Greenham Common, Berkshire
Newtown, Isle of Wight
Porton, Wiltshire/Hampshire
Salisbury Plain Central, Bulford, Wiltshire
Salisbury Plain West, Warminster, Wiltshire
Stanford PTA Norfolk
Yardley Chase, Northamptonshire

With 20–30 butterfly species

Bawdsey, Suffolk
Bridgwater, Somerset
Browndown, Hampshire
Caerwent, Gwent
Castlemartin, Dyfed
Penhale, Cornwall
Portreath, Cornwall
Shoeburyness, Essex
Salisbury Plain East, Larkhill, Wiltshire
West Dean, Wiltshire

---

fumes. Disused airfields naturally sport a carpet of wild flowers and a profusion of butterflies, particularly the skippers and browns. Moths are equally well represented on many military sites and some local counts verge on 300 species. The Duke of Burgundy fritillary (*Hamearis lucina*) is found on at least four military sites in southern England.

Management of habitats as well as catering for the individual requirements of particular butterfly species still goes on at MOD sites. For instance on the grassland expanses of Catterick and Feldom in Yorkshire bracken is controlled by aerial spraying and this has created 285 ha of good grazing land.

Porton Down straddling the Wiltshire/Hampshire border provides a special case study. It is the largest expanse of chalk grassland in Britain with 1,620 ha of chalk on its 2,835 ha site. It sports 18,000 bushes of juniper (*Juniperus communis*) (or 20 per cent of the total population in southern England) on its scrubby wastes, so this represents an enormous playground for butterflies. Plenty of territories may be set up round the bushes, just like the situation one has in many parts of the wilder Continent. The N.C.C. began a long-term investigation of the ecology of butterflies on this precious site. Most of the area had been managed agriculturally 30 years ago and it was interesting to note habitat change and abundance of butterflies. So far, 36 species have been found there, including the locally distributed chalkhill blue and the dark green fritillary.

CONCLUSION

It is a sad day for butterfly-lovers that butterflies are declining. Most of the decline is due to habitat loss engineered by man. We may become wise after the event, but may now be at the stage Rachel Carson was in *Silent Spring* in the 1960s — twenty years after the widespread use of organic insecticides. The effects of long-term adulteration and grubbing-out of so many butterfly havens is now catching us up. We suddenly become surprised and concerned when butterfly populations take a turn for the worse. John Heath astutely observed that a population crash of five million to 50,000 may go un-noticed, but one from 50,000 to 500 will be obvious.

Many of the habits of man which destroy butterflies are done in the name of 'improving' the land. Let us not forget the main reason for this apparent mania to till the earth; the people of the world all need to be fed and no government is likely to conserve butterflies at the expense of feeding mouths. Unproductive, butterfly-rich land is consequently eliminated to make way for intensive agriculture. Unfortunately all the aspects of being a good farmer such as draining the land, ditching and hedge-cutting can be harmful to butterflies. Clearly, removal of hedges and woods and the ploughing of ancient meadows completely destroys the rich wildlife that spent millennia evolving there. The farmers often get a bad press from the conservationists but we must hope that those havens for wildlife set up in recent years on farms — hedgerows, spinneys, ponds and wild woods — provide a refuge for the local butterflies. The specialist butterflies are not likely to do very well in the modern agricultural environment. We must look to the opportunist butterflies, like some of the browns, skippers and some of the nymphalids to colour the countryside of the future. Unfortunately the farmer cannot satisfy conservation demands and always win. Here are some of the methods of farming and some of the policies of farmers which have been responsible for decreasing the populations of certain butterflies: not growing so much lucerne, not managing coppice woodlands, grubbing our coppices, relaxing grazing and too much mowing of meadows. It is incumbent upon us lepidopterists to let farmers know what butterfly species are present on their land. Liaison groups like the UK Farming and Wildlife Advisory Group (F.W.A.G.) do a wonderful job. Unfortunately our task to discover more about the ecological requirements of butterflies has only just begun and some species may slip to extinction before we know much about them at all.

Farmers are not entirely to blame for the decline of butterflies. Urban sprawl consumes an enormous amount of countryside each year and road widening takes away further land and removes hedgerows. A major threat to apollo butterflies in the mountains of Europe are the ski-resort developments, and in the coastal areas around the Mediterranean many other species of butterfly have been killed by tourism developments.

For increased productivity in the food market we have paid the price of losing a major part of one aspect of our living heritage. Innocuous butterflies which once inspired the poets and artists no longer grace large tracts of the European countryside. One has to travel to the unproductive 'bad lands' – uplands, mountains, borders, *causses* and all those areas with poor soils and where governments hardly ever give subsidies – to appreciate the beauty of butterflies and to see them in their natural habitats. Butterflies and intensive agriculture do not mix.

Bibliography

This is not an exhaustive bibliography of books on butterflies. It is impossible to list the numerous scientific papers and theses from which much information and many generalities have been incorporated into this book. For example, the author's book on the large white butterfly (quoted below) contains over 4,000 references which may be of use to students of insect natural history.

The Royal Entomological Society of London (41 Queen's Gate, London SW7 5HU) have published several multi-authored symposium proceedings of which *The Biology of Butterflies* (Academic Press, 1984) is highly recommended; only a few entries are quoted here. Other key works relevant to European fauna include the *Proceedings of the 3rd Congress of European Lepidopterology Cambridge, 1982* which was published by the Societas Europaea Lepidopterologica in 1985 (Erbprinzenstrasse 13, D-7500, Karlsruhe 1) and John Heath's *Threatened Rhopalocera (butterflies) in Europe*. Finally, I must draw attention to volume 7 of *The Moths and Butterflies of Great Britain and Ireland* which should be available in early 1987.

Baker, R.R. (1978) *The Evolutionary Ecology of Animal Migration*, Hodder & Stoughton, Sevenoaks

—— (1984) 'The Dilemma: When and How to Go or Stay' *The Biology of Butterflies*, (eds.) Vane-Wright, R.I. and Ackery, P.R., Symposium of the Royal Entomological Society of London, Number 11, Chapter 26, pp. 279–96

Balletto, E., Lattes, A. and Toso, G. (1985) 'An ecological study of the Italian rhopalocera', *Proc. 3rd. Congr. eur. Lep. Cambs.*, 7–22

Beningfield, G. (1981) *Beningfield's Butterflies*, Penguin, London

Brooks, M. and Knight, C. (1982) *A Complete Guide to British Butterflies*, Jonathan Cape, London

Carter, D. (1982) *Butterflies and Moths in Britain and Europe*, Pan Books, London

Creed, R. (1971) *Ecological Genetics and Evolution*, Blackwell, Oxford

Davies, N.B. (1978) 'Territorial defence in the speckled wood butterfly (*Pararge aegeria*): The resident always wins', *Anim. Behaviour*, 26: 138–47

Dawkins, R. (1976) *The Selfish Gene*, Oxford University Press, London

Dennis, R.L.H. (1977) *The British Butterflies, Their Origin and Establishment*, E.W. Classey, Faringdon

—— (1982) 'Mate location strategies in the wall brown butterfly, *Lasiommata megera* (L.) (Lepidoptera : Satyridae): wait or seek?', *Ent. Rec. J. Var.* 94: (11–12), 209–14; 95: (1–2), 7–10

Douwes, P. (1975) 'Territorial behaviour in *Heodes virgaureae* L. (Lep: Lycaenidae) with particular reference to visual stimuli', *Norw. J. Ent.* 22: 143–54

Dowdeswell, W.H. (1981) *The Life of the Meadow Brown*, Heinemann, London

Feltwell, J. (1976) 'The migration of *Hipparchia semele*', *J. Res. Lepid.* 15: 83–91

—— (1981) 'Observations on the Scarce Swallowtail *Iphiclides podalirius* (L.) (Lep: Papilionidae)', *Proc. Trans. Br. ent. Soc.* 14: 76–81

—— (1982) *The Biology, Biochemistry and Physiology of Pieris brassicae (Linnaeus)*, Dr W. Junk, The Hague

Feltwell, J. and Philp, E. (1980) 'The Natural History of the M20 Motorway', *Kent Field Club*, 82: 101–14

Ford, E.B. (1945) *Butterflies*, Collins New Naturalist Series, No. 1; subsequently published in Fontana paperback in 1975

Fountaine, M. (1980) *Love among the Butterflies*, Penguin, London

Gomez Bustillo, M.R. and Rubio, F.F. (1976) *Mariposas de la Península Ibérica* (3 vols.), Inst. Nacional Para La Conservación de la Naturaleza

Gray, D. (1978) *Butterflies on my Mind*, Angus & Robertson, London

Grey-Wilson, C. (1981) *The Alpine Flowers of Britain and Europe*, Collins, London

Guilbot, R. (1982) *Élevage des Papillons*, Société Nouvelle des Éditions Boubée

Hall, M. (1981) *Butterfly Research in I.T.E.*, Institute of Terrestrial Ecology, Huntingdonshire

Harborne, J.B. (1977) *Introduction to Ecological Biochemistry*, Academic Press, London

—— (ed.) (1978) *Biochemical Aspects of Plant and Animal Coevolution*, Academic Press, London

Heath, J. (1977–) *The Moths and Butterflies of Great Britain and Ireland*, Blackwell, Curwen, Harley Books. 11 Volumes proposed

—— (1981) *Threatened Rhopalocera (Butterflies) of Europe*, Nature and Environment Series no. 23. European Committee for the Conservation of Nature and Natural Resources. Council of Europe, Strasbourg

Heath, J., Pollard, E. and Thomas, J. (1985) *Atlas of Butterflies in Britain and Ireland*, Viking, London

Henriksen, H.J. and Kreutzer, I.B. (1982) *The Butterflies of Scandinavia in Nature*, Skandinavisk Bogforlag. Odense, Denmark

Heslop, I.R.P., Hyde, G. and Stockley, R.E. (1964) *Notes and views on the Purple Emperor*, Southern Publishing Co. Ltd, Brighton

Higgins, L. and Hargreaves, B. (1983) *The Butterflies of Britain and Europe*, Collins, London

Higgins, L.G. and Riley, N.D. (1970) *A Field Guide to the Butterflies of Britain and Europe*, Collins, London

Hinton, H.E. (1981) *The Biology of Insect Eggs*, Pergamon, London

Huffaker, C.B. and Rabb, R.L. (1984) *Ecological Entomology*, John Wiley, Chichester

International Union for the Conservation of Nature and Natural Resources (1983) *The I.U.C.N. Invertebrate Red Data Book*, Gland, Switzerland

Johnson, C.G. (1969) *Migration and Dispersal of Insects by Flight*, Methuen, London

Kettlewell, H.B.D. and Heard, M.J. (1961) 'Accidental radioactive labelling of a migratory moth', *Nature, Lond.* 189: 676–7

Kudrna, O. (1974) '*Artogeia* Verity, 1974. Gen. rev. for *Papilio napi* (Lep. Pieridae)', *Ent. Gaz.* 25: 9–12

Lack, D. and Lack, E. (1951) 'Migration of insects and birds through a Pyrénées pass', *J. Animal Ecol*, 20: 63–7

Lundgren, L. (1977) 'The role of intra- and interspecific male:male interactions in *Polyommatus icarus* Rott. and some other species of blues (Lycaenidae)', *J. Res. Lepid* 16: (4) 249–64

Magnus, D.B.E. (1956) 'Experimental analysis of some "overoptimal" sign-stimuli in the mating behaviour of the fritillary butterfly *Argynnis paphia* L. (Lepidoptera: Nymphalidae)', Proc. tenth Int. Congress of Entomology Vol. 2

—— (1956) 'Experimentalle Untersuchungen zur Bionomie und Ethologie des Kaisermantels *Argynnis paphia* L. (Lep. Nymph.)', *Z. f. Tierpsychologie* 15: 4 397–425

Measures, D.G. (1976) *Bright Wings of Summer*, Cassell, London

Nature Conservancy Council (1981) *The Conservation of Butterflies*, Booklet, 26 pp

Pollard, E. (1977) 'A method for assessing changes in the abundance of butterflies', *Biol. Conserv.* 12: 115–34

Pollard, E., Hooper, M.D. and Moore, N.W. (1974) *Hedges*, Collins New Naturalist Series, No. 58, London

Porter, K. (1984) 'Sunshine, sex-ratio and behaviour of *Euphydras aurinia* larvae', *The Biology of Butterflies* (eds.) Vane-Wright, R.I. and Ackery, P.R., Symposium of the Royal Entomological Society. Chapter 28, pp. 309–11

Rackham, O. (1983) *Trees and Woodland in the British Landscape*, Dent, London

Reader's Digest (1984) *Field Guide to the Butterflies and Other Insects of Britain* (principal consultant and author J. Feltwell) London

Robertson, T.S. (1980) 'An Estimate of the British Population of *Apatura iris* (Linnaeus). (Lepidoptera: Nymphalidae)', *Proc. Brit. ent. Nat. Hist. Soc.* 13: (3/4) 89–94

Rothschild, M. (1970) 'Toxic Lepidoptera', *Toxicon* 293–9

—— (1983) *Dear Lord Rothschild, Birds, Butterflies & History*, Hutchinson, London

Rothschild, M. and Farrell, C. (1983) *The Butterfly Gardener*, Michael Joseph/Rainbird, London

Rungs, C.E.E. (1981) *Catalogue Raisonne des Lepidoptères du Maroc*, Inventaire Faunistique et Observations Ecologique. 11, 2 vols

Russwurm, A.D.A. (1978) *Aberrations of British Butterflies*, E.W. Classey, Faringdon

Schoonhoven, L.M. (1972) 'Plant recognition by lepidopterous larvae' in *Insect/Plant Relationships*. (ed.) H.F. van Emden, Symposium of the Royal Entomological Society of London. pp. 87–99

Shoard, M. (1980) *The Theft of the Countryside*, Temple Smith, London

Shreeves, W.G. (1980) 'Territorial behaviour in British butterflies', *Entomologist's Rec. J. Var.*, 92: 267–9

Smith, C.J. (1980) *Ecology of the English Chalk*, Academic Press, London

Southwood, T.R.E. (1961) 'The number of species of insect associated with various trees', *J. Anim. Ecol.*, 30: 1–8

—— (1966) *Ecological Methods* (2nd edn), Chapman & Hall, London

Stubbs, A.E. (1985) 'Is there a future for butterfly collecting in Britain?', *Proc. Trans. Br. ent. Nat. Hist. Soc.*, 18: 65–73

Thomas, H.M. (1979) *Grandmother Extraordinary*, Stewart Williams, Barry

Thomas, J. (1984) 'The conservation of butterflies in temperate countries; past effort and lessons for the future' *The Biology of Butterflies*, (eds.) Vane-Wright, R.I. and Ackery, P.R., Symposium of the Royal Entomological Society of London. Chapter 33, pp. 333–53

Thompson, D'A.W. (1961) *On Growth and Form*, Cambridge University Press, London

Thomson, G. (1983) *The Butterflies of Scotland: A Natural History*, Croom Helm, London

Tweedie, M. (1977) *Insect Life*, Collins, London

Whalley, P. (1979) *Butterflies*, Hamlyn Nature Guide, Hamlyn, London

—— (1980) *Butterfly Watching*, Severn House, London

—— (1982) *Butterflies*, Mitchell Beazley, London

Williams, C.B. (1930) *Migration of Butterflies*, Oliver & Boyd, London

Williams, C.B., Common, I.F.B., French, R.A., Muspratt, V. and Wilks, M.C. (1956) 'Observations on the migration in the Pyrenees in the autumn of 1953' *Trans. R. ent. Soc. Lond.*, 108: 385–407

Index of scientific names

General index

abdomen 14
aberrations 46
abundance estimates 89–90
admirals 56, 65
adonis blue 88
African grass jewel 43
African monarch vii
Algeria 6, 101
alpine argus 43
alpine flowers 40–2
alpine grizzled skipper 42
amber 2–3
American painted lady 98
androconia 8, 14
androconial patches 12
antennae 7–8
anti-freeze vii, 23, 102
aphrodisiacs 13
apollo vii; collecting 109, 114;
   populations 90; winking 50
Arctic fritillary 39
Arctic grayling 24
Arctic woodland ringlet 119
arguses 93
Arran brown x, 50, 70
arthropods 7
Asian fritillary 39
aspect 59
Assmann's fritillary 21
Austria 2, 109, 112
Azores vii, 6

back to front mimicry 54–6
background matching 20
Baker, Robin 95
Balkan fritillary 39
Balletto, Emilio 107
basking 78
Bates, Henry 4
Bath white 99, 103
Belgium 5, 99
Berger's clouded yellow 43
birthworts vii
black and brown colours 49–50
black hairstreak 20, 68, 77, 110, 118
black satyr x
black-veined white viii, 80, 110
blues, coppers, hairstreaks 10
blue-spot hairstreak 67, 83
bog fritillary 106, 109
boreo-alpine spp. 42
breathing 13
Bretherton, R.F. 95
brimstone viii; cross-pollination 80;
   foodplants 32; introduction 116;
   movement 98; recognition 12

BM (NH) 5
brown arguses 42
brown hairstreak 68
browns 10
brush-footed butterflies 10
buckler mustard viii
Budapest Entomological Society 4
Bulgaria 4–5
butterfly hunters 3–5
butterfly roles 26

cabbage feeders 35–6
Canary Islands vii, 6
cannibals 21
carotenoids 18, 48–9
carrying capacity 86
caterpillars 20–24
chalkhill blue 89
Chalmers-Hunt, M. 95
Chapman's green hairstreak 44
chequered skipper 38, 108
Chovet, Gerard 12
chrysalises 24–5
C.I.T.E.S. 109
cleopatra viii
climate 59
clouded yellows 86
Code for Insect Collecting 109
co-evolution 31, 80
collecting 108–10
coloration 25
comma 28, 73
common blue ix, 93
compound eyes 11
Corsica vii, 5, 99
Corsican swallowtail 109
Courtney, Stephen 58
cranberry fritillary 27
Cretan argus 43
Crete vii, 44
crypsis 25
Cynthia's fritillary 5
Cyprus 5
Czechoslovakia 109, 112

Dalmatian ringlet 106
damon blue 43
Danube clouded yellow 43
dark green fritillary 119
Darwin, Charles 4, 45
Davies, N.B. 58, 94
defensive strategies 20
De La Beche Nicholle, Mary 5
Dennis, Roger 94
De Worms, Charles 6
dewy ringlet 42

130